THIS IS IT!

The complete story of the Great Train Robbery

This is it! For the first time in 50 years what you are about to read - or dip in and out of as time allows - is the most complete and detailed record of what factually happened at the Great Train Robbery. The book also covers the run up to the Great Train Robbery, its immediate aftermath, and what has happened to those involved in the fifty years that have passed since the robbery took place in the early morning of 8 August 1963.

THIS IS IT!

It was the New York Herald Tribune that called the events of 8 August 1963, 'History's greatest robbery', and few would now argue with that. Even Scotland Yard told the Daily Mirror at the time: 'There has never been anything quite so big, bold and crookedly brilliant as The Greatest Train Robbery.'

For many involved, it is a story that takes them from the cradle to the grave. A story that refuses to die, and one that fifty years on still fascinates and entertains a nation.

The information - parts of which are being revealed for the very first time - comes from both sides of track. From the actual people involved in the robbery, both the robbers and their associates, as well as the people who wanted to catch them, have them caught, and lock them away for 30 years. Even shoot them, as was the case with one senior police officer.

The information comes first hand from Bruce Reynolds, the mastermind of the crime and the man who cried 'This is it!' as he saw the train for the first time. It also comes from Ronnie Biggs, the most famous of the robbers and the man who admits that he was the most privileged spectator to the entire robbery.

The relevant information has also been extracted from official police, government and Post Office records, and from the media. This book also clarifies some of the myths and legends that surround the robbery and looks at foul play. Stories that range from the strange and disturbing, to the downright bizarre.

Over the last fifty years a lot of water has flowed under Bridego Bridge, often sweeping away the facts of what actually happened there on the morning of 8 August 1963. So the version of the crime that is so often repeated is normally the one spun by one of the interested parties. Read carefully, and between the lines, and you may be shocked by what you discover.

By the standards of the time, even today, the Great Train Robbery was not a violent crime, although painted as such. Many of those who took part would be the first to admit that they had been involved in many, far more violent crimes over the years, including the London Airport job. A crime for which the sentences for those convicted were just five years. Somehow the Great Train Robbery pricked at the heart of the Establishment and the faceless men in the grey suits who wanted their pound of flesh then, and in the five decades that have passed.

The coshing of the driver, which the robbers have said is regrettable, has been used as a smokescreen with the passing of time to cover other unsavoury elements of the crime and that includes the planting of evidence, the death of an innocent man, and the sentences that could not possibly reflect what the judge, given his track record, could consider as fair.

At times when you read about the Great Train Robbery it appears that the train driver, Mr Jack Mills, was the only victim.

Nobody has looked to see if the early death of Mills' assistant on the train, David Whitby, could have been a result of the robbery. He died from a heart attack in January 1972 at the age of just 34 having been almost totally ignored and abandoned by the railway company and the police following the robbery. Today we might ask if he, and others on the train, suffered from post traumatic stress disorder.

Then there is the story of William Boal. One of the first people arrested for the Great Train Robbery. The police would not listen to Boal's plea that he was not one of the robbers. And although they had Boal and the money, they could not find any proof to link him to Leatherslade Farm. That is until the Yard's forensics team, which was still collecting evidence from the farm even after the public had been allowed to visit the scene, conveniently found some. Yellow paint, on a small watch winder.

Unfortunately for Boal, as you can read in Foul Play the same paint evidence had been planted on some shoes belonging to Gordon Goody, and the police were not going to admit that and let Goody slip away. So for the Yard to get its man, another innocent man was allowed to die in prison with horrific consequences for his family.

The sentences handed down to the robbers by Justice Edmund Davies also do not add up. Or rather they

The robbers. Or are they?

do, to a total of 573 years for the 12 key people on trial. For most of the robbers it was two concurrent sentences, the crimes being: 'robbery - being armed with an offensive weapon' (30 years / 10,957 days) and 'conspire / robbery with violence' (25 years / 9,130 days). 30 years was a tougher sentence at the time than that being given to murderers, child molesters or spies. But clearly Justice Davies thought the sentences to be fair. Or did he?

We can now reveal that on 30 September 1963 - less that two months after the robbery and six months prior to passing sentence on the train robbers - Justice Davies gave his ruling on a case in the court of appeal. The man appealing was Charles Connelly who took part with three other men in the armed robbery of the Royal Arsenal Co-operative Society depot in Mitcham, Surrey in November 1962. During the robbery a van driver, and father of two young children, was shot and killed. At the original trial the man who pulled the trigger was sentenced to death, later commuted to life, which turned out to be 16 years. The other three, who were also armed, were sentenced initially to 15 years each. The judge stating that the gang was 'one of the most dangerous ever to be brought to justice'.

Yet in September 1963 Justice Davies would, at appeal, reduce Connelly's sentence. Noting: 'Gravely reprehensible as his conduct was, this court is of the opinion that the sentence was excessive and should be reduced to ten years.'

It would be interesting to try and explain to the robbers and their families - who were no angels - just how a judge can conclude that ten years is a fair sentence in a robbery that saw a man gunned down in cold blood (he was not even the target of the robbery), yet a few months later he decides that 30 years is the right and fair sentence for a gang of train robbers, and is in no way excessive.

You will read many other such stories over the following pages. Of the robbers not at the track, look out for a certain Brian Field. A gentleman and a lawyer without whom the robbery could never have taken place. Yet in 1964, with the class system still firmly in place, Field saw his sentence at the appeal stage cut from 25 years to 5 years as the judges accepted that no facts had been established that he knew of the intention to stop and rob the train. If that was true, it showed just how little the police and the prosecution actually knew about what really happened, and who was behind the Great Train Robbery.

With the train robbery you can't even believe your own eyes. Many of the iconic photos from the robbery are not what they seem. You may think you have seen a photo of the train at Bridego Bridge after the robbery, only it is not the right train, and it is not on the right track. The actual train was removed from the scene before any photos were taken, and even before the police arrived.

PART ONE

BEFORE THE ROBBERY:
Criminal blitzkrieg - planning and preparation

1913 - 22 October
William Gerald Boal, the train robber who wasn't, is born in Durham.

1920 - 21 February
Jimmy White, the quartermaster, is born.

1921 - 30 May
Roger John Cordrey, the man who knew how to stop a train, is born.

1921 - 17 December
John Denby Wheater is born.

1929 - 12 March
Robert Alfred (Bob) Welch is born.

1929 - 8 August
Ronald Arthur Biggs, the most famous of the robbers, is born in Lambeth, South London.

1930 - 11 March
Douglas Gordon Goody, the firm's managing director and the man in charge on the track, is born in Putney, London of Irish decent.

1930 - 27 April
Thomas William Wisbey is born.

1931 - 27 January
Ronald Christopher 'Buster' Edwards - a familiar name and face from the robbery - is born in Lambeth, London.

1931 - 6 June
John Daly is born in New Ross, Republic of Ireland.

1931 - 7 September
Bruce Richard Reynolds, the robbery's mastermind, is born in Charing Cross Hospital in the Strand.

1932 - 5 March
Freddie Foreman, who will not take part in the robbery, but will help the robbers in the aftermath, is born at 22 Sheepcote Road (now Rowditch Lane) in Battersea, London.

1932 - 30 June
Charles Frederick Wilson, one of the gang's star players and best known, is born in Battersea.

1933 - 8 April
James Hussey is born.

1934
Thomas Marius Joseph Butler - who will become the 'Grey Fox' and head of the Flying Squad - joins the police.

1934 - 15 December
Brian Arthur (Field), a key source of information, is born. Put up for adoption, he is adopted by Reginald and Ivy Field.

1935 - 30 August
Roy John James, a world class racing driver and the fastest of the gang on four wheels, is born.

Bruce Reynolds' mother dies in hospital a few days after giving birth to a daughter. The baby girl dies a short time later. Reynolds is looked after and raised by his father and grandmother.

1936
Biggs family moves around the corner from Dalyell Road to 30 Kimberley Road, London SW9. Biggs goes to school in Lingham Street.

1939 - 17 May
Charmian Powell, the future 'Mrs Biggs', is born.

A generation that survived the blitz

1941 – 26 December
At the Surrey Sessions Roger Cordrey is found guilty of two counts of embezzlement and six counts of falsification of accounts. He is sent for Borstal training. It is the only conviction on Cordrey's record prior to the Great Train Robbery.

1940-42
Due to World War II and the Blitz, many of the train gang are evacuated as children from London. Bruce Reynolds is evacuated to Ipswich, Suffolk and then on to Warwickshire. Ronnie Biggs is evacuated from London to Coombe-in-Teignhead in Devon and Delabole in Cornwall.

Biggs returns to London in 1942 and goes to Stanley Street School and Brixton School of Building. Bruce Reynolds returns to his grandmother's house at 38 Buckmaster Road in Battersea. Bruce and Charlie Wilson live in neighbouring streets in Battersea and go to the same school, but in different years.

1944 - 7 June
Jimmy White is invalided out of the army due to a duodenal ulcer. He had served in World War II with the Royal Artillery Regiment and Army Air Corps.

1946
Due to his eyesight, he wears thick glasses; the Royal Navy turns down Reynolds. He decides he would like to be reporter and gets a job as a messenger in Northcliffe House in Fleet Street, home to the Daily Mail, Sunday Despatch and Evening News.

Reynolds attention is drawn to cycling. A passion he will never lose. He first joins Paris Cycles in Stoke Newington, and then Claud Butler, a Clapham High Street based bicycle dealer and frame builder and became part of their semi professional racing team.

1947 May
Biggs enlists in the Royal Air Force. He signs on for eight years as a regular and four years in the reserves. Posted to Cardington and then Melksham in Wiltshire. Finally to RAF Halton close to Aylesbury.

1948 - 2 March
17-year-old Gordon Goody is sentenced to 21 months and 12 strokes of the birch for robbery with violence.

1948 - 17 September
Bruce Reynolds' first conviction. It is for assaulting a policeman after being stopped for riding a cycle without a light. The policeman had kicked the bike and then Reynolds. He is fined 20 and 30 shillings.

1949-1955
John Wheater, who had been put forward for the Military Cross during World War II, works for the army legal service. He retires with the rank of major.

1949 - 8 February
Biggs' first court appearance as an adult at County of London Sessions. Nine days later, on 17 February, Biggs is sentenced to six months for shop breaking, housebreaking, stealing and using a false ID card. It is his first prison sentence. He receives a dishonourable discharge from the RAF.

1949 - 1 June
Bruce Reynolds given Borstal Training in Wormwood Scrubs for shop breaking and larceny.

1949 - 28 July
Biggs is sentenced to three months in HMP Wormwood Scrubs at the North London Magistrates Court for 'taking and driving away a motor vehicle'. Bruce Reynolds and Ronnie Biggs meet for the first time.

1950
Reynolds and Biggs both end up in HMP Lewes for Young Prisoners. Reynolds is badly beaten up by the guards and thrown in solitary. Biggs organises to get some hot cocoa to Reynolds by swinging a cup from cell to cell. A special friendship is forged between the two men.

1952 - 21 May
Eastcastle Street Robbery. At the time Britain's largest post war robbery. £287,000 (about £6.6 million at 2013 values) is stolen by seven masked men from a post office van in Eastcastle Street, just off Oxford Street. 18 mailbags are stolen. The crime is credited to Billy Hill. Terry Hogan, a close friend of Bruce Reynolds, is said to be involved. No one is ever caught or charged.

Reynolds is called up for National Service. He serves with the Royal Army Medical Corps in Aldershot but goes AWOL after a couple of days. When arrested he slashes his wrists and ends up in hospital.

1952 - July
Bernard Rixon buys Leatherslade Farm, the future hideout for the train robbery gang.

1952 - 19 August
Biggs is released from HMP Lewes and meets up again with Bruce Reynolds.

1952 - December
Reynolds and Terry Hogan rob a White City greyhound stadium bookmaker.

1953
Reynolds and Biggs both end up back in HMP Wandsworth, but now as adults. Reynolds refers to Wandsworth as "an old boys reunion of the elite criminals in the land."

1954
Reynolds and Daly break in and steal a bookmaker's trousers while he sleeps. Their informant is right, as there is £600 in his pockets. About £13,500 at 2013 values.

1955
Bruce Reynolds, John Daly and Terry Hogan become regulars at the Star Tavern in Belgravia. It is also used by the police. Lord Lucan, Diana Dors, Richard Harris and racing driver Mike Hawthorne are among the regulars. As is Billy Hill.

Reynolds refers to 'Tatler' and 'Harpers' as his "trade publications" which he reads to spot potential targets and for news of when people will be out of their homes at social events listed in the calendar.

Reynolds makes the first of many trips to the south of France. He stays at the Hotel Westminster in Nice but quickly discovers the charms of Cannes. He starts thieving along the Riviera most summers. Reynolds and Hogan consider a plan to steal Marie Antoinette's necklace from the Louvre in Paris.

1956
Reynolds starts frequenting the Marlborough in Chelsea that is located in the same street as the police station. Reynolds gets to know Bob Huntley, then a chief detective inspector, but later head of the bomb squad, and Maurice Ray, Scotland Yard's top fingerprint expert.

Freddie Foreman starts working with Buster Edwards and Tommy Wisbey. Also in the gang are Alfie Gerard and Micky Regan.

The Krays, Freddie Foreman, Buster Edwards

1957
Reynolds buys a Porsche, which he crashes in Le Mans. He is now a known name of interest with Scotland Yard.

1957 - 6 June
Reynolds' grandmother, who had raised him, has a major stroke. She dies five days later.

1958 - 7 January
Charlie Wilson is sentenced to 12 months for receiving stolen goods.

1958 - 16 January
Reynolds is charged with malicious wounding with intent and for assaulting a police officer. He is sentenced to 3 years 6 months.

1958 - May
Brian Field is charged with conspiring to cheat and defraud the creditors of Dyne Engineers Co. The case is later dropped due to insufficient evidence.

1958 - 23 June
Jimmy White is sentenced to 18 months for shop breaking and stealing photographic equipment.

1958 - 1 October
Bob Welch is convicted for receiving stolen coffee, tea and custard powder. He is sentenced to 9 months.

1958 - 28 October
Tommy Wisbey is sentenced to 4 months for receiving stolen radios.

1958 - 7 December
Jimmy Hussey is sentenced to 3 years for a warehouse break-in and causing grievous bodily harm with intent to resist arrest.

1959 - 26 May
Charlie Wilson is sentenced to 30 months for conspiracy to steal.

1959 - 6 July
Reynolds is stabbed three times while in prison. Reynolds himself sets up the attack in the hope of getting out of prison early.

1959 - 8 October
The General Election results in a third successive Conservative victory. Harold Macmillan is the Prime Minister. Margaret Thatcher is one of the new Tory MPs.

1960
Reynolds, who has been going out with Rita Allen, comes out of prison and starts going with her younger sister, Frances. John Daly is going out with the middle sister, Barbara.

Bruce and Frances move to Lytton Grove in Putney. Their favourite restaurant is Wheeler's in Duke of York Street, off Jermyn Street. The clubs they frequent include the Astor, Embassy, and Les Ambassadeurs.

1960 - 20 February
Biggs marries Charmian Powell at Reigate Register Office.

Reynolds meets Buster Edwards at Charlie Richardson's club, the Mary Ann, in Peckham. Edwards takes him to meet Gordon Goody at the Castle Pub in Putney. He also gets to know Roy James.

1960 - May
Brian Field is employed by John Wheater as the managing clerk at TW James & Wheater, based at

London in the early 1960's

3 New Quebec Street, London W1. Field is thought to have built up the firm's criminal law business through his underworld contacts. Bruce Reynolds is introduced to Brian Field.

Reynolds, Buster Edwards, Charlie Wilson, Roy James and Terry Hogan rob an armoured van. It takes less than a week to go from an idea to the fruition of the crime.

They have a guard on the inside and the robbery takes just three minutes to complete. The amount stolen is over £60,000 (over £1.1 million at 2013 rates). The guard is paid £8,000 (£150,000) as his share.

1960 - 23 July
Nicholas Grant Biggs is born at Redhill County Hospital. Biggs moves to 37 Alpine Road in Redhill.

1960 - August
Nine mailbags containing £7,000 (£132,000 in 2013) are stolen from a train on the London to Brighton line.

1960 - 20 September
Six mailbags containing £9,000 (£170,000 in 2013) are stolen from a train on the London to Brighton line. The train is stopped at Patcham Tunnel, Preston Park, by a rigged signal.

1960 - 9 December
The first episode of 'Coronation Street' is aired.

1960 - 31 December
Last day a farthing coin is legal tender.

1961
John Daly moves to 73 Burleigh Road in Sutton.

1961 - 20 January
John F. Kennedy is sworn in as the 35th President of the United States of America.

1961 - 8 March
Edwin Bush is arrested in London for a stabbing. He is the first criminal in the UK to be identified by Identikit.

The method of stopping a train by fixing the lights is used to rob a train on the Waterloo to Teddington line in London.

1961 – April
A mailbag containing £15,000 (£275,000 in 2013) is stolen on Brighton Station by robbers disguised as railwaymen. Yuri Gagarin becomes the first man is space.

1961 - July
Reynolds badly crashes his car in Arles in the south of France while driving from Cannes to Pamplona for the running of the bulls. He is kept in hospital for some time and nearly loses an arm.

1961 - August
Construction of the Berlin Wall.

Bruce and Frances Reynolds, Barbara and John Daly

Terry Hogan, Bruce Reynolds, 1962

Wedding of Mr and Mrs Biggs, 20/2/1960

Reynolds in the south of France

Wedding of Bruce Reynolds, 7/9/1961 (L to R front): Roy James, Barbara Daly, Terry Hogan, John Daly, Micky Ball, Bruce and Frances Reynolds, and "friends".

The early 60s, especially 1963, would not be all fun and games for Prime Minister Harold Macmillan

1961 - 7 September

Reynolds marries Frances Margaret Allen at Kensington Registry Office. Having moved out of Lytton Grove prior to the summer in France, they move in to a flat on Putney Hill.

1962

The core of what will be the Great Train Robbery gang, with Bruce Reynolds in charge, plan a number of robberies involving trains, but not stopping them. The first target is the Irish Mail train from Paddington that Edwards has been told about by an informant. Reynolds and Goody recce the train and see that the security is heavy at both ends of the route, but not on the train itself. A train that carries passengers as well as goods.

The target of the robbery, a wage shipment for railway workers in Swindon, is transported every Tuesday.

The plan is to stop the train close to West Drayton in West London by pulling the communication cord. The gang, travelling as passengers, would then break into the guard's van and steal the boxes holding the wages. A van would be waiting trackside to whisk them away.

The first trial run goes to plan. The actual train robbery, however, is pure Keystone Cops. A fiasco after the train does not stop in the expected place and goes on for a further half a mile. The gang has to abandon the payload and the take from the robbery and the risk is just £700 (£12,000 in 2013).

1962 - 2 January

The first episode of *Z Cars* is aired on the BBC. Spike Milligan releases *Wormwood Scrubs Tango*.

1962 - 6 January

John Daly marries Barbara Allen, making him Bruce Reynolds' brother-in-law.

1962 - 20 January

Brian Field marries Karin Klemich, a German, at St Marylebone Register office. They met at Winston's nightclub in 1961. Karin will admit in an article published after the trial in Stern' that she knew many of the robbers prior to the robbery.

1962 - 26 January

The Daily Express uses as the headline "Great Train Robbery Foiled" for a story about a botched raid on a train in Essex. The target is thought to be a Travelling Post Office.

1962 - 22 March

Nicholas Rufus Reynolds is born. At the time Reynolds is planning to steal the Rothschild's jewels.

1962 - 25 March

Jimmy and Sheree White move into a house at 66 The Woodlands, Beulah Hill in Croydon.

1962 - 4 April

James Hanratty is hanged at Bedford Prison for the murder of Michael Gresten.

1962 - July

Reynolds comes up with a plan to steal pools coupons and money that is picked up from a chain of betting shops and taken by train to William Hill's office in central London.

Reynolds grabs a bag with £3,000 (£52,000 in 2013) in it from Redditch Station. They then follow the vans in London, which can contain up to 30 bags, but the plan is abandoned when Reynolds learns that these bags are mainly full of cheques and not cash.

1962 - 11 July

First live television broadcast between the US and UK. The following night the Rolling Stones give their first performance at London's Marquee Club.

1962 – 13 July

After a disastrous by-election result in Orpington, the Prime Minister sacks seven of the cabinet.

1962 - August

A mailbag robbery takes place on a Victoria to Brighton line. The robbers distract the guards by starting a fire on the train. National Provincial Bank robbery in Clapham. Charlie Wilson is one of the suspects.

Wilson receives information about how the wages

London Airport job

Bandits drove round perimeter road and out of disused gate to Staines-road

Cars waited here and drove off down one-way street after the raid

Bandits got out of lift in foyer as money arrived

Bandit cars parked here before raid

for BOAC are handled at London Airport. It involves the wages, expected to be close to £300,000-400,000 (£5-7 million in 2013), being driven a couple of hundred yards from a branch of Barclays Bank to Comet House, BOAC's maintenance headquarters. Reynolds, Goody and Edwards visit Comet House and observe the transfer. They decide the best place to snatch the wages is not on the street, but in the actual foyer of Comet House.

The plan includes everyone looking like City gents. Some would go to the toilet at the top of the building and hold the lift until they saw the delivery being made. Other gang members would be in the lobby; they would be able to surround the security guards as they wait for the lift. Fast cars were waiting outside for the getaway. "People think twice about questioning a gentlemen," Reynolds would say.

1962 - 5 October
The first James Bond film, *Dr No*, opens in the UK, and the Beatles release their first single, *Love Me Do*. The song will be performed in the film *A Hard Day's Night* (1964) with the band sitting in the guard's compartment of a train.

1962 - 14-28 October
Cuban Missile Crisis threatens world peace.

1962 - 20 November
First attempt at the London Airport robbery is called off due to an unusual police presence on the day.

1962 - 27 November
Key members of Bruce Reynolds' train robbery gang pull off the London Airport robbery at Comet House. The raid starts at 9.45 am and takes just 5 minutes to complete. A £62,500 BOAC payroll, about £1 million at 2013 values, is stolen. The value, however, is less than the gang had been expecting.

After the robbery, a high-speed car chase takes place around the airport's perimeter fence and spills on to the A30. The gang escape in two stolen Jaguars thanks to the driving skills of Roy James and Micky Ball. One of the Jags has been stolen in Eaton Square from American actor Craig Stevens, then best known for playing TV detective Peter Gunn. Both Jags are found abandoned in Hounslow

Reynolds, Goody, Edwards, Wilson, White, James, Mickey Ball, Terry Hogan, and Harry Smith take part in the robbery.

1962 - 28 November
Thinking that the police may be looking for him, Bruce Reynolds leaves for Paris and then moves on to Tangier. Mary Manson ("Cockney Mary") is visited by the police and asked if she has seen her friends Reynolds and Goody.

1962 - 29 November
Wilson, Goody, James and Ball are arrested for the airport job but not charged. There is a police line up at Cannon Row police station, opposite Scotland Yard, but none of the gang is picked out.

1962 – 4-6 December
Severe smog in London. Visibility at times is less than 5 yards. Bus services are suspended and thousands of cars abandoned across London.

1962 - 12 December
Police hold more identity parades at Twickenham

police station for the airport job. Goody and Ball are picked out and are charged. Brian Field, of James and Wheater Solicitors, is asked to help defend Goody.

1962 - Mid December
Frances Reynolds visits Mary Manson and asks her to look after 9-month-old Nick. She travels to meet up with Reynolds in Paris for Christmas.

1962 - 18 December
Jimmy Hussey is sentenced to five months by a Munich Court for picking pockets. He is deported to the UK on 19 December. Because he was under arrest, Hussey probably missed taking part in the airport job for which Wilson had invited him.

1962 - Late December
Ball decides to plead guilty at the trial. Goody pleads not guilty. Ball is sentenced to 5 years for a crime that turns out to have been far more violent than the Great Train Robbery. Goody has Brian Field tamper with the jury and the evidence. The Old Bailey jury finds Goody and Wilson not guilty. Terry Hogan pays a police contact £1,500 (£25,000 in 2013 values) to have Reynolds' name removed from the case file.

1962 - 26 December
While hauling the up Midday Scot, D326, an English Electric Class 40 diesel locomotive, runs into the back of the Liverpool - Birmingham Express between Winsford and Crewe at Coppenhall Junction. 18 passengers are killed and 34 injured. D326 (later renumbered '40126') is the engine that will be involved in the Great Train Robbery.

1963
According to estimates in the year of the Great Train Robbery, the Post Office was moving over £4,000 million around the country annually, much of it by train.

1963 - January
The big freeze of 1963. One of the coldest winters on record, with temperatures below freezing for over two months. From 22 December 1962 to 5 March 1963 there are no frost-free nights in the UK. Even the sea freezes off the coast of Kent. At Hampton Court, the Thames could safely be crossed on the ice.

Bruce and Frances Reynolds

Bruce and Frances Reynolds move from Paris down to the south of France. Other key gang members are now back in London after being found not guilty at the airport trial.

Reynolds and the gang start considering trains again. First consideration is the weekly gold train that runs from Southampton to Waterloo that normally carries a ton of gold that has been shipped from South Africa by Union Castle. Security, however, is very tight. Plus there is the challenge of having to move the heavy gold bars.

Reynolds turns his attention to the 'Money Train' that runs from Bournemouth to Waterloo with a last stop at Weybridge. After observing the train a plan is developed to snatch the bags from Weybridge station in the early hours. The load is normally between 27 and 32 bags on a good night. These are then taken from the train at Weybridge, not loaded on to it as Reynolds first thought. From the station they are taken to the Post Office in Weybridge. The best place for an ambush, the gang believe, is the station itself.

With the plan in place, and the equipment needed sourced, fate plays a part as the stolen getaway cars

Members of the airport gang and wives

to be used in the robbery are themselves stolen from Jimmy White's garage with some of the key equipment.

Evenings out in London for some of the gang at the Embassy Club and Astor with Reynolds, Edwards, Goody, Daly, Wilson, Hogan, as well as wives and girlfriends. Mary Manson is also present.

1963 - 11 January
Summer Holiday, starring Cliff Richards, receives its London premiere. The single tops the charts on 16 March and again on 6 April.

1963 - 14 January
The Flying Scotsman locomotive makes its last scheduled run.

1963 - 23 January
Double agent, Kim Philby, defects.

1963 - February
Brian Field, having returned from visiting Germany with his German wife, contacts Gordon Goody with information about a very large regular transfer of money by Travelling Post Office. They meet at the Old Bailey.

There is a second meeting of Field with Goody and also Buster Edwards at the offices of Wheater. This new information makes this train a priority over the 'Money Train'.

1963 - 14 February
Following the sudden death of Hugh Gaitskell, the Labour Party elects Harold Wilson as its new leader. Opinion polls show that Labour would win an election. The Conservatives have ruled since 1951.

1963 - 21 March
Bob Welch is convicted at Bow Street Magistrates Court on four counts of selling intoxicating liquor outside permitted hours. He is fined £210. In the US, Alcatraz Federal Penitentiary is closed.

1963 - 24 March
Christopher Dean Biggs is born at Redhill County Hospital. Biggs plans to buy Alpine Road.

1963 - 27 March
The chairman of British Railways, Dr Richard Beeching, issues a report calling for huge cuts in the UK rail network. It includes the closure of 2,000 stations and the loss of 68,000 jobs. Many rail workers, and the unions, are not happy.

1963 - March onward
The planning and preparation for the Great Train Robbery starts proper. Brian Field introduces Gordon Goody and Buster Edwards to an informant in Finsbury Park. The man becomes known in the story of the Great Train Robbery as the 'Ulsterman'. Over time he becomes an almost mythical figure.

The target of the robbery is to be the Glasgow to Euston Travelling Post Office, also known as the 'Up Special' or 'Up Postal'. The informant says there could be up to £6 million on the train (over £100 million at 2013 rates). All the high value packages on the train originate from banks along the route and are being transported to the East Central District Post Office in King Edward Street, London EC1, close to St Paul's.

A meeting takes place with Reynolds, Wilson, Goody, James, White, Edwards and Mary Manson to discuss the chance of pulling off the job. One concern is that the job could be a police set up to trap them all for the London airport job.

Reynolds and Daly take a train ride along the route out of Euston. The best place to stop the train, they conclude, looks to be open countryside around the Leighton Buzzard area, about 40 miles from Euston Station by train or road.

A meeting is held at Edwards' flat (214 St Margarets Road) in Twickenham. The gang realise that they will need to stop the train, but without being on it as it is not a passenger train. Edwards has heard of the success of South Coast Raiders in stopping trains and knows and has worked with one of the gang, Tommy Wisbey.

Edwards meets Wisbey at a bar owned by Bob Welch. 'Mr Three' is also there. This is followed by a further meeting at Waterloo Station to introduce Roger Cordrey, head of the South Coast Raiders, to Edwards and Goody. A subsequent meeting takes place at Edwards' flat for Reynolds to talk in more detail with Cordrey and Wisbey.

1963 - 8 April
At the 35th Academy Awards, 'Lawrence of Arabia' is named best picture.

1963 - 19 April
Bill Boal is fined £10 (about £175 in 2013 values) and bound over for 12 months at Mortlake Magistrates' Court for assault on a policeman.

1963 - 24 April
An Austin goods platform truck is sold at auction of ex-War Department vehicles to a contractor in Edgware. He subsequently sells the truck on to Jimmy White.

1963 - 28 April
Roy James wins his race at Snetterton.

1963 - 1 May
A key date in the history of the Great Train Robbery and those involved. In court "1st May 1963" is chosen as the legal start of the "conspiracy" that is the Great Train Robbery.

A full meeting of the train robbery gangs takes place. At the time this includes Reynolds, Goody, Wilson, Edwards, White, James, Daly, Cordrey, Wisbey, Welch, Hussey and the three unnamed robbers.

After a series of further reccces by Reynolds, Cordrey, Daly, Wilson, Edwards and James, the track running through the countryside outside of Leighton Buzzard is chosen as the best location for the robbery. In May 1963, Reynolds and Daly visit Glasgow to see where the train starts.

1963 - 19 May
Roy James wins his race at Brands Hatch.

1963 - 30 May
Bruce Reynolds is fined £10 (about £175 in 2013) at Ongar Magistrates Court for poaching.

1963 - June
James and White visit Royal Oak (Ranelagh Bridge), the main train depot for Paddington. They find the Night Flyer and walk through the deserted and ghostly train passing through the sorting office and into the High Value Package (HVP) coach.

The gang also check out a new more secure HVP coach that is coming into service. The new coach is not seen as a major problem, other than it may take a short time longer to break into. A meeting of the gang is held as a friendly football kick-about on Wimbledon Common.

On a boozy night out in London, Reynolds and Goody find themselves at Euston Station next to a train parked up on the siding. They decide to see how difficult it is to get it to move. They do get it to move, but find it more difficult to stop. It moves slowly forward at 3 mph. Reynolds and Goody abandon ship and in the morning check the papers to see if the incident has made the news. Both men are more convinced than ever that they must have a professional backup train driver for the robbery.

Due to cost of his second child Ronnie Biggs, a builder in Redhill, asks his good friend Reynolds for a loan of £500 (£6,000 in 2013). Reynolds can't loan Biggs the money, as all his spare cash is now focussed on the train robbery.

Bruce and Frances (and their son Nick) visit Ron and Charmian Biggs. It is the first time that Biggs hears of the robbery. Reynolds discovers that Biggs is working for a train driver who is due to retire shortly. Reynolds and John Daly visit Biggs a few days later to check on the train driver. Biggs is invited by Reynolds to be part of what will become the Great Train Robbery. He is to supply the backup train driver for the job.

Goody and Edwards meet again with the 'Ulsterman'.

Biggs is introduced to the gang at Roy James' flat at 907 Nell Gwynn House in Chelsea. Biggs notes: "I have to say they looked a pretty formidable bunch. With a few exceptions they were all big men and even though they were well dressed the majority still had the distinctive look of villains."

Biggs is voted on to job although James votes against. He believes he will be able to drive the train if required and sees the driver as a possible weak link if things go wrong and he is arrested.

Biggs takes 'Peter', his train driver, to Euston to check on the type of train he will need to drive. Peter establishes that pressure is needed for the breaks to be released and for the train to move. He is happy that the train is not that different from the type he is used to.

Options are discussed for what to do after the robbery. Roy James' suggestion is to have a fleet of Jags and for the gang to drive them quickly back to London straight after the robbery with the money.

Due to concerns about the attention that a fleet of jags may create at night, and the fact that there would be no control over the money and what was in each car, it is decided to find a local hideout where the money can be sorted, counted, and split into the shares, the 'whacks'.

1963 - 3 June

Roy James wins his race at Snetterton. He also wins on 8 June at Aintree, 22 June at Goodwood, 23 June at Cadwell Park and 13 July at Oulton Park.

Roy James, top driver

1963 - 5 June

John Profumo, Secretary of State for War, resigns over his affair with Christine Keeler. Three days later osteopath Stephen Ward, who introduced Keeler to Profumo, is charged with living off immoral earnings. Keeler is also reputed to be the mistress of a Soviet Spy, William Vassall. Profumo's downfall, however, is lying to the House of Commons. The impact of the Profumo Affair is that the polls show Labour would easily win a General Election.

During the coverage of Profumo, two journalists are sent to prison for the allegations that they had made in articles regarding the Civil Lord, Tam Galbraith, and Vassall. The case did not endear the government to Fleet Street.

1963 - 13 June

Roy James, the gang's main getaway driver, is fined £15 (about £255 in 2013 values) and ordered to pay £15 costs in the County of London Sessions for dangerous driving.

1963 - 18 June

Henry Cooper fights Cassius Clay (later Muhammad Ali) at Wembley. Clay, after being knocked to the ground, wins when the fight is stopped in the 5th round.

1963 - 24 June

Bruce Reynolds visits Midland Marts Estate Agents in Bicester to look for a possible "hideout" and base for the gang. He visits Leatherslade Farm in the parish of Oakley, Buckinghamshire.

Two miles from the Oxfordshire border, the main buildings at Leatherslade Farm sit 300 yards back from the main road, the B4001 or Thame Road, close to the villages of Brill and Oakley, between Bicester and Thame. At the time it is either not shown on Ordnance Survey maps or listed as 'Nuthooke Farm'. Locally it is known as "Rixon's place".

1963 - 26 June

President John Kennedy makes his "Ich bin ein Berliner" speech in West Berlin.

1963 - 27 June

Wheater and Brian Field visit Leatherslade Farm. An offer is made on the property to its owner Bernard Rixon. Initially the offer is not accepted. Rixon's family have owned the farm since July 1952.

1963 - July

Jimmy White organises the uniforms and overalls needed for the robbery, and with Mr One he organises the transport. An ex-War Department Land Rover (BMG 757A) is sold on 2 July to a London motor dealer. Charlie Wilson starts to organise the food and drink that will be needed.

Drivers, lead by Roy James, test the route using the back roads between Bridego Bridge, south of Leighton Buzzard, and Leatherslade Farm.

A low-key rehearsal takes place at Stewarts Lane, Nine Elms, Battersea. Final roles are decided for the robbery. All the roles are interchangeable in case someone is missing or incapacitated on the day. Everyone is told to make their own arrangements for after the robbery.

1963 - 12 July

16-year-old Pauline Reede is murdered in Gorton, Greater Manchester. She is the first known victim of the Moors Murderers, Ian Brady and Myra Hindley. The killings continue through October 1965 when the couple are finally arrested.

1963 - 21 July

A Land Rover to be used in the robbery is stolen by Jimmy White from Oxenden Street, London WC1 between 7.30 and 11 pm.

1963 - 23 July

Leatherslade Farm is purchased for the gang via Leonard Field for £5,550 (about £95,000 in 2013 values). The owner agrees that after the payment of a 10% deposit, a cheque for £555 drawn on the account of James & Wheater, the 'buyer' can occupy the farm immediately.

Payment for the balance will not need to be made until 13 August. 7% interest is to be paid on the balance to cover Rixon's mortgage on his new property.

1963 - 26 July

An ex-War Department Land Rover is purchased from a London motor dealer for £195 (around £3,300 in 2013 values). The number plate is BMG 757A. This will also be used on the stolen Land Rover.

1963 - 29 July

Completion of the purchase of Leatherslade Farm. The Rixon family moves out of the farm but leave some items behind in the kitchen, including a blue-edged Pyrex dish.

The keys are left with Mrs Lillian Brooks, resident of The Bungalow, Thame Road, Oakley. The keys for the farm are picked up at 3.30 pm. Jimmy White moves out of his house in Croydon.

1963 - 30 July

Jimmy White purchases an Austin goods platform truck from a government surplus contractor in Edgware.

1963 - 31 July

Goody and Edwards hold a last meeting with the 'Ulsterman' and Field. The date of the robbery is set for the early hours of Wednesday, 7 August.

The 'Ulsterman' says that the gang need not be concerned about the new design of HVP coaches, as they will not be being used on the train.

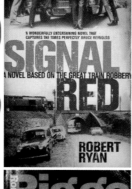

RONALD BIGGS

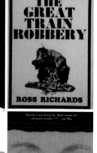

THE GREAT TRAIN ROBBERY

ROSS RICHARDS

SIGNAL RED

A NOVEL BASED ON THE GREAT TRAIN ROBBERY

ROBERT RYAN

THE BIGGS TIME

RONNIE AND MICHAEL, MAN AND BOY

Michael Biggs

WITH NEIL SILVER

Killing Charlie

WENSLEY CLARKSON

Biggs

a novel that draws on the true events surrounding the Great Train Robbery

Keep on Running

The most wanted man

Colin Mackenzie

SLIP-UP

ANTHONY DELANO

NIPPER READ

The Man Who Nicked the Krays

LEONARD READ

with James Morton

RONNIE BIGGS

ODD MAN OUT: THE LAST STRAW

THE GREAT TRAIN ROBBERY

HISTORY-MAKING HEIST

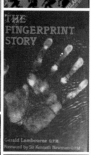

THE FINGERPRINT STORY

Gerald Lambourne Q.P.M.

Foreword by Sir Kenneth Newman Q.P.M.

GREAT TRAIN CRIMES

Murder & Robbery on the Railways

Jonathan Oates

RONNIE BIGGS

HIS OWN STORY

THE TRAIN ROBBERS

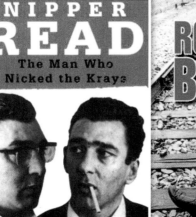

PIERS PAUL READ

Author of ALIVE

The compelling story of the man who masterminded the Great Train Robbery

The Autobiography of a Thief

BRUCE REYNOLDS

THE TRAIN ROBBERS

Ex-Detective Superintendent MALCOLM FEWTRELL, former Head of Bucks CID in charge of investigating the Great Train Robbery

RONALD BIGGS

ODD MAN OUT

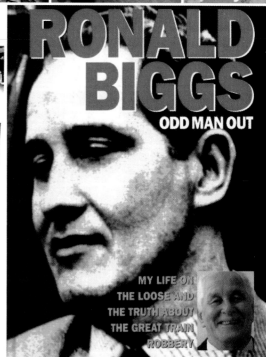

MY LIFE ON THE LOOSE AND THE TRUTH ABOUT THE GREAT TRAIN ROBBERY

TELL THE INSIDE STORY OF
THE GREAT TRAIN ROBBERY

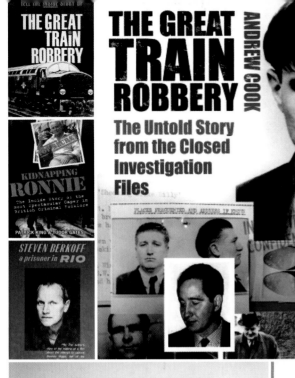

KIDNAPPING RONNIE
The Inside Story of the most Spectacular Caper in British Criminal Folklore
PATRICK KING & TUDOR GATES

STEVEN BERKOFF
a prisoner in RIO

THE GREAT TRAIN ROBBERY
ANDREW COOK
The Untold Story from the Closed Investigation Files

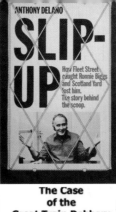

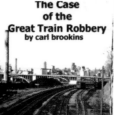

ANTHONY DELANO
SLIP-UP
How Fleet Street caught Ronnie Biggs and Scotland Yard lost him. The story behind the scoop.

The Case of the Great Train Robbery
by carl brookins

à sean sean detective story

The Robbers' Tale
the real story of the great train robbery
PETA FORDHAM

The Great Train Robbers: Ronnie Biggs, Buster Edwards, Bruce Reynolds

Books LLC

The Great Train Robbery
the inside story
the century's most startling crime
WITH NEW AND HITHERTO UNPUBLISHED MATERIAL — BY-EX SCOTLAND YARD DET. SUPT. JOHN GOSLING AND FAMOUS CRIME WRITER, DENNIS CRAIG

'THE MOST BLOOD-CURDLING GANGSTER MEMOIR YOU'LL EVER READ.'
THE NEWS OF THE WORLD

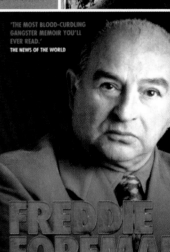

FREDDIE FOREMAN
THE GODFATHER OF BRITISH CRIME

PHOTOCOP
The Man who photographed the Great Train Robbery
The Biography of John Bailey A.R.P.S, A.P.A. G.B

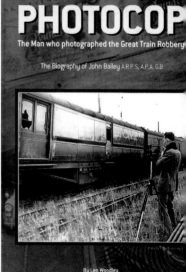

By Len Woodley

THE GREAT TRAIN ROBBERY FILES

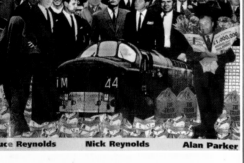

Bruce Reynolds   Nick Reynolds   Alan Parker

BRUCE REYNOLDS
Crossing the Line: The Autobiography of a Thief
The compelling life story of the man who masterminded the Great Train Robbery

NO FIXED ADDRESS:
THE GREAT TRAIN ROBBERS ON THE RUN
BY EX-DETECTIVE CHIEF SUPERINTENDENT FRANK WILLIAMS

THE GREAT BRITISH TRAIN ROBBERY, 1963

BIGGSY'S BIBLE

CRIME ARCHIVE

The Great Train Robbery

SLIPPER OF THE YARD

JACK SLIPPER

NODDY IN TOYLAND
MR PLOD AND THE TRAIN ROBBERS

Ronnie Biggs

The Odd Man Out: 50 Years On the Ron

Let's put the record straight. I was not the 'brain' behind the Great Train Robbery. That honour goes to my dear friend Bruce Reynolds, who we sadly lost at the start of 2013. Neither was I the 'tea-boy'. Although I like to think I was the best cook out of all sixteen at Leatherslade Farm.

If I am famous it is not for what I did on the morning of 8 August 1963, but because I went over the wall of the Hate Factory in July 1965 and kept on running until I returned to Britain under my own steam (and with a little help from my friends), nearly forty years later.

Many, many stories have been told about the robbery and the robbers since 1963. Stories that have included everything from a German SS connection to a Mr. Big linked to the government of the day. I have read that I shot the driver in the head, and I am still accused of having coshed the driver, despite not even being on the train at the time.

The truth was rather different. By reading this publication you will learn what happened at the Great Train Robbery, as well as the stories behind some of the secrets and lies. Many of these facts and stories are being revealed for the first time, so don't say you weren't told or warned. Read with care - and between the lines - and you will get a much clearer picture of what actually went on.

The train robbery, as the police finally cracked, was the labour of two London gangs who came together for the 'Big One'. I was a member of neither gang. I was on the rail embankment that night because of my friendship with one man, Bruce Reynolds. That, plus the building work that I was doing at the time on the house of a train driver. I believe in fate, and fate played a big part in getting me involved in what is still the world's most famous robbery.

I first met Bruce in Wormwood Scrubs prison in July 1949. From the start it was clear that Bruce was a cut above the other cons. We became good friends and discovered a mutual interest in music, literature and breaking the law. Our paths crossed several times during the ensuing years - in and out of prison - but we never got up to any villainy together prior to the train robbery itself, or after.

So when I called Bruce in June 1963 to try and borrow £500 (about £6,000 today), the last thing I had on my mind was returning to a life of crime, and certainly not trying to stop and rob a train. The only trains I knew about were the ones that ran between Redhill and London, and they never seemed to be on time.

After the call to Bruce, the rest is history. Yes, I could have stepped away as Bruce had offered me a lump sum for simply getting him the driver, but I wanted the buzz of being involved, and that was

Ronnie Biggs.
A Rio landmark.

Ronnie Biggs and his son, Michael

There was the sound of glass shattering as the assault team lead by Charlie (Wilson) got to work. Peter and I sat in awed silence witnessing the sacking of the train with the military precision that Bruce demanded. The gang worked swiftly, passing the mailbags by way of a human chain to the truck. Even then I knew that I was a spectator to an historic moment, although I did not appreciate just how historic it was going to be. The Great Train Robbery was now fact and, like it or not, I was part of it.

For the want of a few quid fifty years ago, I had plunged headlong into an enterprise that was to lead me into almost forty years of a life 'on the run' and ten years locked up behind bars. Had I heeded the advice I was given back in 1963 things might have turned out very different.

I might have spent the rest of my life freezing my nuts off on some bleak building site somewhere in Britain. So, if you want to ask me if I have any regrets about being one of the train robbers, I will answer, 'NO!' I will go further: I am proud to have been one of them. I am equally happy to be described as the 'tea-boy' or 'The Brain'. I was there that August night and that is what counts. I am one of the few witnesses – living or dead – to what was 'The Crime of the Century'.

Although I have said that I have no regrets about being a train robber, I do have regrets about the crime itself. It is regrettable, as I have said many times, that the train driver was injured. During Jack Slipper's visit to Brazil we spoke about Mills and his injuries, and Mr Slipper voiced the opinion that the coshing amounted to 'unnecessary violence'. I agreed with him, but I pointed out that the driver was only struck once, and by mistake, and not 'beaten repeatedly, with blows from an iron bar and left broken and bleeding beside the railway track', as I had read in the papers at the time of my capture in 1974, and often since.

Mills was not the only victim. The people who paid the heaviest price for the Great Train Robbery are the families. And that is the families of all the people involved in the Great Train Robbery. The robbers' families, the families of Old Bill, the families of the railmen and post office workers, and even the families of the people that have helped us over the years. All have paid a price, one way or another, for our collective involvement in the robbery. A very, very heavy price, in the case of my family. For that, I do have my regrets, but it has still been a life well worth living.

something I was not getting from my building work. The money would also come in handy, especially as Charmian had just given birth to our second son!

As it turned out, a £5 each-way bet placed on a couple of nags on the eve of the robbery saw me win exactly the same amount of money I had asked to borrow from Bruce. I could have backed out again, but I was not going to let Bruce down. He had his reasons for inviting me on the job, and it wasn't just about our friendship. Bruce was far too professional for that.

One of my tasks at the robbery was to look after our back up driver, Peter, and that meant I ended up in the privileged position of watching the robbery unfold. Once we had moved the train from Sears Crossing to Bridego Bridge - and Peter could have done it, given time - he and I sat in one of the Land Rovers. From our position we had a clear and unobstructed view of the bridge and the paralyzed train.

PART TWO

THE GREAT TRAIN ROBBERY:
Midnight ramblers - what actually happened at the robbery

1963 - 1 August

Bruce Reynolds and Frances move out of their flat on Putney Hill.

1963 - 2 August

Goody flies to Northern Ireland with his mother and a friend to establish an alibi.

1963 - Sunday, 4 August

The Searchers *'Sweets For My Sweet'* tops the charts in the UK on the week of the train robbery, although some charts, including the BBC's, credit Elvis Presley's *'(You're the) Devil in Disguise'*.

1963 - Monday, 5 August

Summer Bank Holiday Monday. After some heavy, thundery rain, the weather improves across the southeast for the holiday. Biggs takes his family to Brighton. A £10 bet on the horses wins him over £600 on an accumulator, but the bookie, Inkpen, has a £500 limit (£8,500 in 2013 values). Biggs has won the same amount of money that he has asked to borrow from Reynolds.

Roy James sets a circuit lap record in his car at Aintree.

On the eve of leaving for the robbery Frances Reynolds stitches officers' crowns on Bruce's uniform as well as the winged dagger on his SAS beret. Frances will spend the time that Bruce is away at a holiday caravan in Winchelsea on the Sussex coast. She will be with her sister Barbara, who is married to John Daly. Jimmy White owns the caravan they will stay in.

1963 - Tuesday, 6 August

Biggs and "Peter" travel by train from Redhill to meet Reynolds for breakfast at a café in Wilton Road, next to Victoria Station. The time is 8 am. Also waiting at Victoria Station are John Daly, Jimmy White and Mr One.

Gordon Goody returns to London from Belfast having bought a single ticket in the name of McGonigil.

The group from Victoria arrive at Leatherslade Farm mid-morning in one Land Rover driven by John Daly. Leatherslade Farm is located 300 yards off the B4001, the Thame Road, close to the villages of Brill and Oakley, between Bicester and Thame.

Biggs and Mr One cook lunch for the group. White fixes a generator while Peter sunbathes in the garden.

Part of the gang turn up in the afternoon in the Austin truck driven by Mr Two. The group includes Tommy Wisbey, Jim Hussey, Bob Welch, Buster Edwards and Mr Three. Welch gets them to stop en route in Bicester to stock up on ten pipkins of ale. Fingerprints on the pipkin, that holds seven pints, lead to his conviction. One of the pipkins is kept in the New Scotland Yard crime museum.

Charlie Wilson and Roy James arrive at the farm in the second Land Rover. Roger Cordrey turns up at the farm later, under his own steam. To pass the time some of the gang play Monopoly that Daly has brought with him to the farm. Wilson is the big winner.

Having returned from Northern Ireland, Goody goes to the house of Brian and Karin Field near Pangbourne (Kabri, Bridle Path, Whitchurch Hill, Berkshire) to wait for the update from the informant. From the news they receive about the Travelling Post Office's High Value Package load that night, Goody and Field decide to postpone the robbery for 24 hours.

Goody arrives at Leatherslade Farm at around 11 pm. The Fields' house is about a one-hour drive away

Leatherslade Farm

from the farm. As he arrives the gang is trying on uniforms and preparing to leave for the raid within the next couple of hours. Goody, who Biggs says was swigging from bottle of whisky, tells them all that they can stand down for 24 hours.

1963 - Wednesday, 7 August – EVE OF THE ROBBERY

Biggs cooks breakfast for the gang. Unbeknownst to Biggs, his older brother, Jack, has died overnight. Charmian calls Redhill Police Station and asks the police to look for Biggs who she believes is 'tree felling in Wiltshire.' The call is logged and will destroy Biggs' alibi.

Reynolds reminds the gang to show as little movement as possible around the house. Everyone, despite the nice weather, is told to stay inside the house unless going to the outhouse, 30 yards from the back of the house.

Roland Wyatt, a neighbouring farmer, calls at Leatherslade Farm in the hope of meeting the new owner so that he can negotiate the use of one of the fields. Reynolds, who meets him outside the house, tells him that they are just the decorators and a 'Mr Fiedling' of Aylesbury is the new owner and will not be around for several days.

Brian Currington, a tractor driver from a neighbouring farm, passes one of the Land Rovers with three men in it at the entrance to the farm. He claims later to have seen the Land Rover on three occasions.

From his description and other information, the police come to believe that one of the three to be Henry Smith of 262 Fieldgate Mansions in Stepney. A man, who although suspected by the police, is never charged.

Late afternoon Reynolds goes over the plans one last time with the entire team.

The Glasgow to Euston Travelling Post Office, Up Postal, consisting of an engine (English Electric Class 40 diesel locomotive - D326 [40126]) and five coaches leaves Glasgow for London at 6.50 pm The train is scheduled to arrive at Euston Station in London at 3.59 am on 8 August. The second coach from the engine is known as the HVP coach (High Value Packets).

The Up Postal arrives at Carstairs, 28 miles south of Glasgow, at 7.32 pm where four coaches that had left Aberdeen at 3.30 pm are added to the back of the train. It departs at 7.45 pm. The engine and nine coaches arrive at Carlisle at 8.54 pm where three further coaches are added. It departs at 9.04 pm There are just 30 HVP mailbags on board the train at this stage.

As dusk falls on the night of 7 August the gang sit around in the dark swapping stories and dirty jokes. Gordon Goody quietly slips out of Leatherslade Farm at around 10 pm to find the local phone box and call Brian Field. The job is confirmed. The night's load of HVP mailbags is expected to be high.

The train stops at Preston from 10.53 to 11.03 pm and leaves with 41 HVP mailbags on board; and at Warrington from 11.36 to 11.43 pm. At Warrington there are still only 46 HVP mailbags on the train.

1963 - Thursday, 8 August – THE GREAT TRAIN ROBBERY [RONALD BIGGS' 34th BIRTHDAY]

It is a cool, dry, moonlit summer night with just a few scattered clouds. Most importantly there is no sign of rain.

The Night Flyer, Up Postal arrives at Crewe Station at 12.12 am on the morning of Thursday, 8 August and leaves at 12.30 am with Jack Mills and David Whitby now in charge of the engine. Both men live in Crewe. The train now consists of the engine and 12 coaches. The coach marked POS 30204 is the HVP coach. 91 HVP mailbags are now in place.

Just before 1 am the gang leaves Leatherslade Farm dressed as an army unit on night manoeuvres. Reynolds has given all the gang a number so that no names need to be used. Reynolds does a count to make sure nobody is missing and all are present and accounted for. Reynolds is number one.

John Daly drives the first Land Rover with Reynolds, Biggs, Peter and Cordrey.

Roy James drives the second Land Rover with Mr Two, Gordon Goody and Jimmy White. In between the Land Rovers is the truck driven by Mr One with Edwards, Wilson, Wisbey, Welch, Hussey and Mr Three.

The route to the site of the robbery covers mainly

'C' class roads through the countryside north of Aylesbury. Only one person is spotted en route, and that is a solitary hitchhiker. But it is the hitchhiker who will be key in reporting to the police his sighting of an army convoy of three vehicles. Another witness spots the three vehicles on the Cublington - Aston Abotts Road travelling towards Aston Abotts at around 1.20 am. That time is probably early.

Sorters Joseph Ware and John O'Connor join the train at Tamworth at 1.23 am and settle into the High Value Packets (HVP) carriage. The train leaves Tamworth at 1.30 am with Frank Dewhurst in charge of the HVP carriage. Also in the HVP van are Leslie Penn and Thomas Kett. There are now 125 HVP mailbags on board.

At around 1.45 am, after a 50-minute, 27-mile drive from Leatherslade Farm, the gang arrives at Bridego Bridge (Bridge 127) in the parish of Mentmore in Buckinghamshire. Bridge 127, two miles south of Leighton Buzzard, takes the rail track over a quiet country road west of the B488, two miles north of Cheddington Station.

At Bridego Bridge the gang swap their army uniforms for overalls to appear as track workers if spotted by passing trains, of which there will be a number. All will wear balaclava-type masks during the assault on the train.

The stretch of railroad at Bridego Bridge consists of four sets of tracks. Two "up" and two "down". Down fast is the track to the west, up fast is the next track, then down slow, and to the east, up slow. The train will be travelling on the up fast track.

Markers are placed at Bridego Bridge to show the driver where to stop. James, Daly and Reynolds cut local telephone wires that link two nearby farms, Rowden Farm near Bridego Bridge and Redborough Farm near Sears Crossing, to the outside world. They also cut the wires of the trackside phones.

The train arrives at Rugby at 2.12 and departs at 2.17 am It now has the full compliment of 128 HVP mailbags on board.

At around 2.40 am, Daly is dropped by Reynolds at

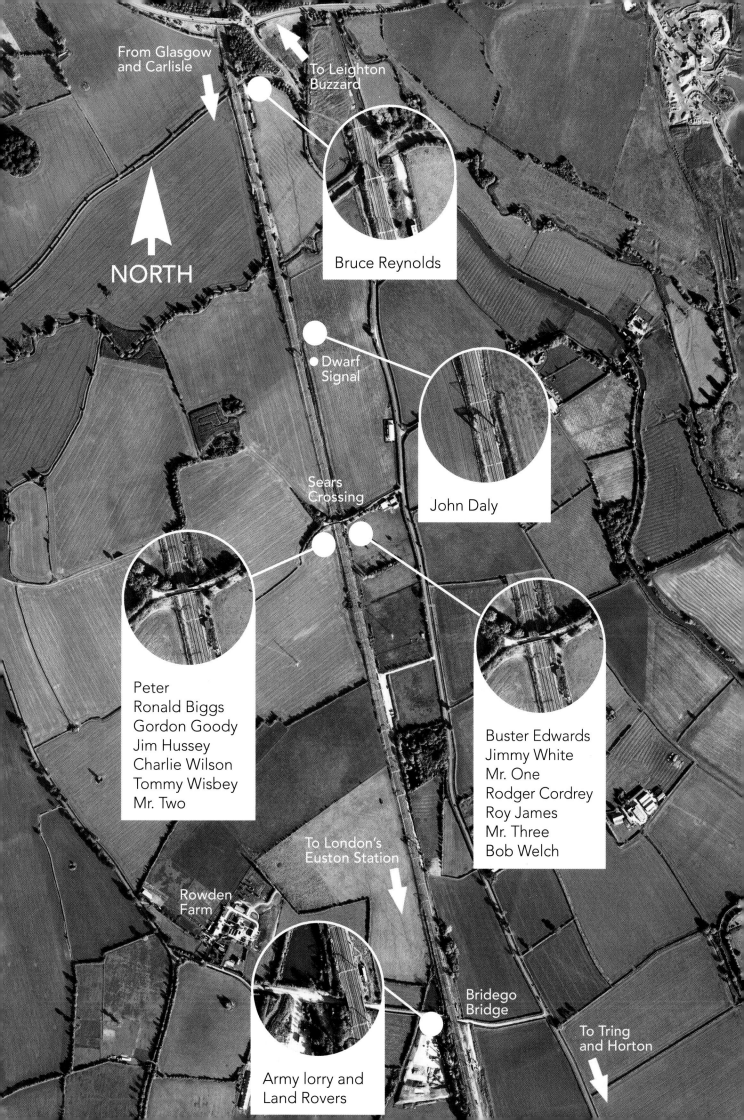

From Glasgow
and Carlisle

To Leighton
Buzzard

NORTH

Bruce Reynolds

Dwarf
Signal

John Daly

Sears
Crossing

Peter
Ronald Biggs
Gordon Goody
Jim Hussey
Charlie Wilson
Tommy Wisbey
Mr. Two

Buster Edwards
Jimmy White
Mr. One
Rodger Cordrey
Roy James
Mr. Three
Bob Welch

To London's
Euston Station

Rowden
Farm

Bridego
Bridge

To Tring
and Horton

Army lorry and
Land Rovers

the dwarf signal (a signal placed at a lower elevation than the others) to prepare to change the signal from green to amber for the up fast track. Roger Cordrey prepares the main signal, where the train will stop, to signal red. This is 1,300 yards on from the dwarf signal. Daly and Cordrey use gloves to cover the green light and four six-volt Ever-Ready Dry cell batteries to keep the amber and red lights shining.

Reynolds is to act as the look out for the train from a high piece of land just 800 yards south of Leighton Buzzard. A spot from where he can enjoy a fine Montecristo No 2 cigar as he waits for the train and his destiny.

Cutting the wire. German reconstruction

Edwards, White, James, Welch, Mr One, Mr Three and Cordrey are to the east of track at Sears Crossing, a bridge that goes over rather than under the track. There will be two tracks (up slow and down slow) between them and the stopped train. The track telephone, located in the middle of the tracks, has had its wires cut.

Goody, Wilson, Wisbey, Hussey, Mr Two, Peter and Biggs are to the west of track at Sears Crossing. There will be one track (down fast) between them and the train. The train is registered as passing through Bletchley at 2.53 am.

At 3 am Reynolds can already see the train coming through Leighton Buzzard, lighting up the sky as it rushes towards him. He warns the gang that the train will soon be upon them. They have been at the track for nearly an hour and a half.

"This is it! This is it! This is it!" Reynolds cries into his walkie-talkie. The response from the team is 'Check.' 'Check.' 'Check.'

Jack Mills slows the Night Flyer, Up Postal as he sees the amber light at the dwarf signal and brings the train to a halt at Sears Crossing. The time is 3.03 am on the morning of 8 August 1963. The train is 38 miles north and short of its final destination of London's Euston Station.

There are five sorters in the HVP carriage (Frank Dewhurst, Leslie Penn, Thomas Kett, Joseph Ware and John O'Connor), and a further 72 sorters spread through the rest of the train under the control of a Post Office inspector. Stops are normal along the route, so there is no reaction from the 77 Post Office workers.

Fireman David Whitby leaves the cab on the left hand side, stepping down between the up fast and down slow tracks. He looks for a trackside phone to call and check why the train has been stopped. These phones are located between the up fast and down slow tracks. He calls back up to Mills: "The wires have been cut".

As Whitby heads back to the cab he sees a figure between the second and third coach, who he thinks is a trackside worker. It is Buster Edwards. He says nothing but beckons Whitby to follow him across the down slow and up slow tracks to the east embankment. He is then grabbed by Edwards and bundled down the embankment where two other gang members are waiting. A hand is put over his mouth and he is shown a cosh. "If you shout, I'll kill you," he is told. Whitby tells the assailant: "You are all right mate. I am on your side."

The locomotive engine is now stormed. Buster Edwards and Gordon Goody are the first of the gang to try to enter the cab. Mills, who had been looking at the train's controls, lashes out at Edwards who, having crossed two sets of tracks, is entering on the left side of the cab where Whitby had left the cab. Goody, who has entered from the right hand side having crossed the down fast tracks, grabs Mills from behind and turns him. Mr Three, who has followed Goody into the cab, coshes driver Mills on the back of the head.

Mills falls sideways to his knees from the blow, striking his head against a solid steel cab wall. Blood pours from the cut. Wilson enters the cab from the same side as Goody and attempts to stop the bleeding with his handkerchief. Mills is moved to the passage leading to train's boiler room. He is told not to look around. Whitby is brought up from the embankment and across the track. He is also put in the passage. He remembers a handcuff being put on his left wrist.

The train robbery gang now control the locomotive, but there is still much work to be done. Biggs is called by Goody from trackside and enters the cab with Peter.

At 3.10 am the signalman from Cheddington signal box telephones Leighton Buzzard signal box to ask where the train is. James and White start to uncouple the locomotive and first two carriages from the rest of the train.

An express train whistles past on the inside down fast line, nearly taking James and White, who are uncoupling the carriages, with it. Thomas Kett, in the HVP coach, hears the noise of the uncoupling and the passing train. Although such mishaps are a frequent occurrence, he thinks they should let the driver know. Being in a sealed carriage he makes use of the only means they have of getting in touch with the driver. They pull the communication cord in the HVP coach. This applies the vacuum brakes, freezing the heavy locomotive to the tracks.

Goody gives Peter, now in the driver's chair, the order to move the train forward. Peter does not react. He knows the pressure needs to build to release the breaks. He is also unaware that the train is one of two that has had a new vacuum system fitted. Goody, impatient to get the train moving, pulls Peter from the chair and tell the gang to 'fetch the driver'.

He puts Mills into the driver's seat and threatens him with a cosh if he does not drive the train.

Mills rectifies the vacuum brake valve by opening the large ejector in order to clear the air fully from the vacuum pipes and lift the brakes. Thomas Miller, the guard at the very back of the train, later notes that he had heard the breaks go on and had seen the vacuum gauge in his compartment drop to zero.

Mills later tells the police that the necessity for taking the action suggested to him that a coach had been uncoupled and that the disconnected vacuum pipe had been returned, but the stopper had not been fixed back properly.

Jimmy White also admitted that when the train did not move he dropped back down on to the track and raced to the back of the two carriages where he discovered the air pressure valve was not fully closed. He kicks it into the shut position and the train starts moving.

The diesel finally lurches into life and begins to roll slowly forward leaving the rest of the train stranded behind. The engine, HVP carriage, and one other carriage are now detached from the rest of the train and are moved south to Bridego Bridge. The time is 3.14 am.

Reynolds, who has picked Daly up in the Land Rover, has seen the train stop from the road and the assault commence. They continue on to Bridego Bridge.

James, riding on the outside of the engine, sees the marker at Bridego Bridge first and tells Mills, through Goody, to stop.

As the train stops at Bridego Bridge the assault starts on the HVP coach. Time, Reynolds has warned, is key. Biggs is told to take Peter to sit in the Land Rover and watch the rest of the robbery unfold. Mills is taken back into the passage and handcuffed to Whitby.

The assault team on the HVP coach is lead by Charlie Wilson and includes Hussey, Goody, Welch, Edwards, Wisbey, Mr One and Mr Three. The post office sorters, aware now that something out of the

The engine and HVP carriage at Cheddington Station

ordinary is happening, try to barricade the sliding main door with the mailbags. They report that they hear the gang say: "They are barricading the doors. Get the guns." There are no guns at the Great Train Robbery, just coshes and axes.

Charlie Wilson and Jimmy Hussey enter the HVP carriage through a broken window, the rest enter through a rear gangway door after storming it. In less than a minute, the side door is open and the HVP mailbags start to emerge.

Mills and Whitby are taken from the locomotive and still handcuffed to each other are put on the west embankment.

They are told to lie facedown. Mills and Whitby smoke a cigarette and remark later that they had to walk through the men already unloading the train.

A chain of men move 120 bags containing 636 high value packets from the HVP carriage, across the down fast track and down the embankment to the lorry. Eight bags, because of time, are left behind. The end of the human chain is Hussey and Welch who are packing the lorry.

40 minutes after stopping the train at Sear's Crossing, and just 24 minutes since stopping the train at Bridego Bridge, Reynolds calls a halt. The time is now 3.40 am.

Mills and Whitby are quietly moved from the embankment and helped in to the HVP coach where they join the five HVP sorters who are lying on the floor. Wilson asks Mills and Whitby if they want any money for their troubles, they decline. "I'll get your

address when this is all over, and send you a few quid," Mills quotes them as saying.

Wilson tells the group of sorters: "Stay here for half an hour, we shall be back." Wilson and Reynolds then check that everyone has been accounted for and that nobody has been left behind. The gang remove their overalls to return to military uniform for the return drive.

The slow return to Leatherslade Farm begins. The gang retrace their steps, travelling west from Bridego Bridge past Mentmore Park and along the C49 and C37 through Ledburn via C75 and C76 to Wingrave, then via the C8 and C71 to Cublington and Whitchurch. The convoy then takes the C57 off the A413 to Quainton via Oving and Pitchcott, and the C25, C30, C75 and C112 to Kingswood. Then the C3 and C60 to Brill and on to the B4011 Thame road. The route is 28 miles.

About 30 minutes after the gang had left the scene Thomas Miller, the guard from the back of the 10 carriages left at Sears Crossing, reaches the engine and HVP coach. Walking in the other direction he has not seen Kent and Penn. He stops a train on the 'Up' slow line. The fireman from this train drives the train and the two coaches on to Cheddington Station. They arrive at 4.15 am.

Pictures published later in the media of a train at Bridego Bridge are not of the train involved in the robbery. The engine in the photo is the D221. The police never inspect the engine and HVP coaches at the site of the robbery.

Dawn is breaking and the gang is already well on the

The coaches left behind at Sears Crossing

way back to Leatherslade Farm. Both Reynolds and Biggs remember them singing along in their Land Rover to Tony Bennett's *The Good Life*.

Scotland Yard receives a call at 4.24 am from the Control Office at Euston saying that Cheddington signal box is requesting the attendance of police and an ambulance. Buckinghamshire Constabulary is informed. At first Scotland Yard believes it is a break in at Cheddington Station.

A witness living on the Brill Road later says she saw the convoy pass her house around 4.30 am heading in the direction of Brill.

The first police arrive at Cheddington at 4.35 am. At the time of the crime the Buckinghamshire Constabulary has 716 officers on its payroll, yet only seven sergeants and 48 constables are actually working when the robbery takes place. Many still do not work over that crucial first weekend as the force is concerned about overtime costs.

On arrival at Chedddington, Mills and Whitby are taken by ambulance to the Royal Buckinghamshire Hospital in Aylesbury. Whitby has no injuries, but he is handcuffed to Mills. Mills is found to have a number of lacerations to his head and 14 stitches are inserted. Although he never loses consciousness, the hospital decides to detain Mills overnight for observation.

The gang arrive back at Leatherslade Farm at around 4.40 am turning left off the B4011. They hear on a police radio that a "Train has been stolen". The truck backs up close to the farmhouse door. The mailbags are moved into farm. The truck is then hidden in a

lean-to-shed, squashing a can of yellow paint in the process. It is starting to get light.

Malcolm Fewtrell, Head of Bucks CID arrives at Cheddington at 5 am. At 5.08 am the first policeman, Inspector Mellows, arrives at the actual scene of what will shortly be known as the Great Train Robbery

It takes Reynolds, Biggs and Mr Two three hours to unpack the money and help sort the 'wheat from the chaff'. Goody checks for homing devises. Cordrey and Wilson act as the accountants. Coshes are hung up on hooks by the door. Peter makes tea for "his boys." Another Monopoly game gets underway for those not working. Others try to grab some sleep.

Reynolds remembers that it is Biggs' birthday and wishes him all the best. Bruce thanks everyone in the gang individually before catching some much-needed sleep. Buster Edwards is asked to wake him in two hours.

At 6.30 am two officers of the Fingerprint and Photographic Department of the Buckinghamshire Constabulary arrive at Cheddington to examine the attacked portion of the train. The engine is already missing, having been taken back to Crewe. They later move on to Bridego Bridge.

BBC Radio's first news broadcast about the robbery goes out at 8 am. It says: *"A Glasgow-to-London mail train was stopped and robbed in Buckinghamshire early today. It happened at Cheddington, near Tring, at about 3 am. The driver and fireman were attacked and injured; and two coaches of the train were detached. They contained mail of all kinds, including registered post. A police spokesman said a short time ago that it's believed a large number of men took part and that they got away with a considerable amount. Neither the driver nor fireman was badly hurt. Every senior officer of the Buckinghamshire police force has gone to the scene of the robbery."*

At 8.30 am Detective Constable Keith Milner from Bucks CID arrives at Bridego Bridge. The first thing he sees is the material marker left by the gang. Fewtrell is still at Cheddington Station where his team is taking statements from the nearly 80 sorters on the train. From Mills, Whitby and the HVP sorters' statements, the police estimate that there were around 15 hooded men involved. It will turn out to be 16.

Embankment steeper and higher than imagined

Despite the BBC Radio news report about the robbery, the first official clarification that Scotland Yard has that it is a train robbery only reaches them at 10.33 am. Nearly seven hours after the robbery.

By noon police say on the radio that they believe the hideout is '30-miles or a 30 minute drive' from Bridego Bridge. An incident room is set up at the headquarters of Buckinghamshire Constabulary in Aylesbury.

At Bridego Bridge the police collect evidence - a bloody cloth, the coupling. But clues are very few and far between. No fingerprints and no tyre tracks are found. By lunchtime it is clear that the Bucks force does not have the necessary resources. Fewtrell advises his chief constable to call in Scotland Yard. First newspaper report ('Evening Standard') suggests that £1,000,000 has been stolen.

Final tally from the robbery is £2,631,784 of which only £343,448 is ever recovered. (First official figure was £2,595,997.10s) Police only have the serial numbers of just 15,000 of the £5 notes, or £75,000.

The take of the Great Train Robbery at 2013 sterling rates is around £46 million.

The accountants split the money into 17 equal "whacks" of approximately £147,000. Just over £2.5 million at 2013 rates. Each share is bigger than the biggest ever pools or lottery wins in the UK at the time

15 "whacks" are for the 15 robbers at the track and one "whack" is for the Ulsterman with one to be split by Brian Field between himself John Wheater and Leonard Field. There is also £40,000, or about £700,000 at today's values, for Peter.

At 10.33 am a general alert about the robbery is sent to police forces in Bedfordshire, Berkshire, Hertfordshire, Oxfordshire and Northamptonshire. "120 mail bags containing a very considerable sum of money are missing," it notes.

The gang already starts the process of clearing up the farm and wiping down all surfaces and disposing of the rubbish. Knowing from radio traffic that the police may be looking for an army truck, Jimmy White starts to paint the Austin a yellow colour. White had planned to take all the empty mailbags and rubbish away in the truck to dispose of them. Burning paper in the kitchen and in the garden causes too much smoke, so the empty mailbags for are thrown down into the cellar.

A witness is to later say that at around 2 pm on 8 August, while driving between Ashendon and Brill, he saw a Vauxhall motorcar and a six-wheel lorry facing each other on the road. A man got in the lorry and a woman entered the car. A second man walked across the field towards Dorton. The witness says he could identify the man walking across the field as Roy James.

At 3 pm a meeting is held at the GPO Headquarters in London of all interested parties. Present are senior officials and officers from Scotland Yard, Buckinghamshire Constabulary, British Transport Police, and various GPO and government departments. After the meeting Detective Superintendent Gerald McArthur of the Flying Squad heads to the crime scene.

Roger Cordrey leaves Leatherslade Farm during the afternoon to cycle 20 miles into Oxford to get the newspapers and check out the lay of the land. He is to return on Friday morning. In Oxford Cordrey books himself into a boarding house run by Mrs Ida Pope and calls his children and then Billy Boal, who he asks to meet him in Oxford on Friday with transport.

Postmaster General, Reginald Bevins, the Conservative MP for Liverpool Toxeth, returns from his family holiday to face the media. The Post Office immediately offers a £10,000 reward for information. Later in the day an extra £25,000 reward is added by Hart & Co, the London loss adjusters for the British Linen Bank and the National Provincial Bank.

Reynolds encourages everyone at the farm to wipe the place down again. "No dabs are to be left". It leads the gang to suggest to Reynolds that he should open up a dry-cleaners with his money!

Hot and difficult to sleep, as plans to leave the farm are put in place some of the gang have been awake for 36-hours.

1963 - Friday, 9 August
THE DAY AFTER ROBBERY

Police set up a series of road checks around the area of the robbery at exactly the same time as the robbery on the previous day in the hope of asking regular travellers if they had seen or noticed anything the night before.

The morning newspapers are now calling the crime "The Great Train Robbery." They also point out that since Reginald Bevin took over as Postmaster General in 1959 there has been eight major robberies of mail carried by train. The Daily Mail goes as far as to say that the police had already been tipped off that a train robbery in Bucks was imminent, while the Daily Sketch goes with the headline "Balaclava and the 40 Thieves."

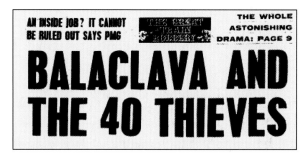

The Daily Mirror, which says that Scotland Yard is already comparing the crime to the Eastcastle Street Robbery of 1952, ends its coverage of the robbery on 9 August by stating: "The Yard men agree, there has never been anything quite so big, bold and crookedly brilliant as The Greatest Train Robbery."

The gang awake early on Friday morning. The "cleaners" get to work again straight after breakfast. BBC Radio news quotes the police once more as saying that they are certain the train robbers are still in the area and within 30 miles of the crime scene.

Mary Manson, who also uses the name Macdonald, (209 Mitcham Lane, Streatham, London SW16) buys a black Austin Healey at the Chequered Flag Sports Cars in Chiswick. The cost is £835 (around £14,000 at 2013 values) and is paid for in cash in £5 notes. During the trial Manson will be considered "a tower of strength and kindliness to the wives and children of the robbers involved in the case."

For extra security the plan is to call in the 'dustman' to take care of the farm after everyone has left. A collection is made and Brian Field will be given £28,000 to get somebody to clear up farm. Police believe the dustman would have been an associate of Reynolds and Daly, William Still, but Still had been arrested on 25 June.

Reynolds and Daly leave the farm and head to nearby Thame to meet Mary Manson and Rene, and to organise more transportation. Roger Cordrey returns with the newspapers and a car.

The gang members start to leave the farm with their respective cuts from the robbery. Cordrey, White, and Mr Two leave in one car. Jimmy White buys an Austin Healey from Allery & Bernard in the Kings Road, London SW3 for £900 paid in cash in £5 notes, and returns later in the day to pick up Mr One.

Reynolds arrives in Thame where Mary Manson and Rene are waiting with a van and the Austin Healey. They make their way back to the farm, Reynolds telling Mary and Rene not to leave the van. As dusk falls Reynolds arrives at the farm. His and Daly's share is loaded and hidden in the van that Manson will drive back to Mitcham, dropping Peter off on the way.

Reynolds takes Biggs and his share in the black Austin Healey. They follow the van as far as Horley. Biggs calls Charmian to say he is on his way home. Charmian asks him if he is in "the company of a friend who wares spectacles."

Farewell takes place between Reynolds and Biggs at Biggs' house in Redhill. They would next meet 29-years later in Rio de Janeiro. After Bruce's has gone Charmian has to tell Biggs about the death of his brother, 15 years his senior, and that she had contacted the police.

After dropping Peter in Redhill, Reynolds goes to the lock-up in Mitcham to check that everything is okay with their whack. He and Daly then go to the Coq d'Or in London to celebrate. Caviar, chateaubriand and good claret.

Late in the evening Brian and Karin Field arrive at Leatherslade Farm to help Goody and Edwards. They return to Field's house (Kabri) close to Pangbourne. Other gang members also go to the Kabri. They include Wilson, Welch, Hussey, Wisbey and Mr Three. Later in the evening, neighbours of the Fields are woken by the coming and goings of motor vehicles. A van leaving at midnight. A dark blue VW dormobile is also spotted.

Karin Field has claimed since that she drove Roy James first to Thame, but as there was no late train, she had to drive him on into London. She returns home only at around 2 am.

Leatherslade Farm has been abandoned.

1963 - Saturday, 10 August

The newspapers with little or no news to report about the robbers, ask questions about why three "bandit-proof" vans were all out of action on the night of the robbery, breaking down between 22 June and 1 August. It is felt that the robbery would not have been successful if one of the vans had been in use.

Reynolds did know of the vans, but nothing was done to sabotage them as the gang felt it would just take a little longer to break in to them. Postmaster General, Reginald Bevins, is convinced that the gang had inside information.

Looking to find a different angle the Daily Telegraph claims that the detectives know who the mastermind is and that he lives in one room in Brighton. He is a miser and is being watched by the police.

Rewards offered for information now stand at £260,000. The highest ever offered in the UK. Hart & Co and Toplis & Hardy, City of London loss adjusters, have offered £200,000 of behalf of a number of banks. Midland Bank has offered £50,000, and the Post Office £10,000. The money is to be paid to the first person giving information that leads to the apprehension and recovery of the money. Banks losses are National Provincial, £1,064,000; Barclays, £500,000; Midland, £500,000; National Commercial, £320,000; Westminster, £50,000; and Bank of Scotland, £11,000.

Reynolds and Daily drive to Winchelsea on the Sussex coast in Daly's Jaguar to be reunited with their wives. Having abandoned their house in Putney, Reynolds first stays at the Hilton on Park Lane and then moves to a flat in Queensway owned

by a friend. Reynolds had a rule: "When in doubt, go first class." This is based on the fact that the fancier the place, the fewer questions you get asked.

Police records show that at 12.30 am on 10 August, they were given the name of Bob Welch as one of the possible robbers. A police informant also tells the police that in January 1963 he was approached to become a member of the gang.

Detective Superintendent John Cummings, of Scotland Yard's Intelligence Unit, says that he was contacted by an informer known as 'Micky' within 12 hours of the robbery and given the names of Reynolds, Daly, Wilson, Welch, Wisbey and Hussey. It has been speculated that "Micky" was Michael Kehoe. Something that has been dismissed by members of the gang and the underworld.

Two days after the robbery, the engine is finally returned to Cheddington from Crewe. DC Keith Milner and Dr Holden examine the interior of the cab and remove blood samples from the window and a ledge. Blood on the ledge backs up the version that driver Jack Mills was indeed struck from behind, and could have then hit his head on the instrument panel as he fell. Mills is discharged from Royal Bucks Hospital.

The police start to interview the 180 members of the Berkhamsted & District Angling Society who fish at a pond by Bridego Bridge. They hope that the robbers may have fished at the pond to observe movements on the track. Cordrey was a fisherman, but denied ever having fished at Bridego Bridge.

Some wives and girlfriends drive to Field's house. Gang members, with the exception of Goody, leave the house in Pangbourne and start to plan where to hide and "bank" their cash. Some of the gang head to London's West End to celebrate. Bill Boal rents a flat for Cordrey in Wimborne Road in Bournemouth.

The Great Train Robbery is still the dominant story on the TV and radio and in all the newspapers, this despite the fact that Dr Stephen Ward, a key figure in the Profumo affair, is buried this day after taking an overdose to avoid going to prison.

1963 - Sunday, 11 August
The Sunday People makes the link between the train robbery and the London airport job. The airport raid is seen as a 'curtain-raiser' for the train robbery and a way to fund it. In fact Reynolds personally funds the Great Train Robbery.

The briefing of 80 uniformed and CID personnel takes place. The police search thirteen key locations close to the robbery site. From another tip, the police believe that the hideout is owned by a man who deals in horses, and that it is on the outskirts of Aylesbury. Police also consider that the robbery might be work of the IRA to raise funds.

The police issue a message to police operating in the region of the robbery: "The attention of all foot and mobile patrols is drawn to the fact that the money may be moved at night, either in bulk or in part".

Jimmy White buys a caravan at the Clovelly Caravan Site, Bexhill Road, Boxhill in Surrey for £325 (about £5,500 in 2013 values). He gives his name as Mr Ballard.

An informant tells Detective Inspector Robert Densham of Oxfordshire County CID that it may be worth the police looking at "Rixon's place" (Leatherslade Farm), as it would be a good spot for a hideout. The farm should have been 'cleaned' by now.

1963 - Monday, 12 August

At 9 am the police finally speak to owner of Leatherslade Farm. Rixon, who is now living in Dunaden, Berkshire, explains that he has recently sold the farm.

Farm worker, John Maris, a herdsman of Glencoe House, Oakley, calls the police about a lorry at Leatherslade Farm. The call is one of over 400 calls logged in Aylesbury that Monday.

Maris had been away on holiday from 26 July to 4 August. From 4 August he saw nothing of note happening at the farm, but after reading in the Monday newspapers that the police were interested in isolated farms he took a closer look at Leatherslade Farm and saw the curtains were drawn and a large lorry, which he had not seen before, was parked in the barn.

The police finally get to take possession of the clothes that the driver, Jack Mills was wearing at the time of the attack. Mills tells the press that he now thinks there were between 20 and 30 men in the gang at the track. "The raid was very well organized," Mills says, "just like a military operation. No orders were given, everyone had their own station, and knew their particular jobs."

Goody buries some of his money under concrete slabs in the garden of his mother's house in Putney (6 Commondale Road, London SW15). Biggs is back at work at his building company in Redhill. All the talk in the pubs is about the robbery.

The police ask local estate agents for a list of properties that have been sold or rented in the past six months and that are within 30 miles of Cheddington.

Jimmy White, his wife, Sheree, and son, visit their new caravan. Witnesses see them with a number of cases that they unload from their car.

Bill Boal rents a lock up garage in Emsbury Avenue in Bournemouth. He also buys a Ford Anglia, a garaged Rover, and an Austin van.

Detective Superintendant Gerald McArthur is made

Yard chief Hatherill announces . . .

WE'VE FOUND THE GANG'S HIDEOUT

Supplies left at the farm

responsible for reports and paperwork on the train robbery case and Detective Chief Superintendant Tommy Butler, the Grey Fox, is brought in to head up the overall investigation. Butler sets up an incident room in New Scotland Yard staffed by the Flying Squad.

1963 - Tuesday, 13 August

The morning papers speculate that the robbery is the work of a criminal mastermind.

The farm worker, John Maris, persists and calls the police again. Leatherslade Farm is finally visited by PC John Woolley and Sergeant Blackman at 10.50 am.

"We found the farm pretty much as they had left it," Woolley recalled. "Their vehicles were still in the yard, their foodstuffs in the kitchen, and the cellar was full of empty mailbags, overalls and masks."

Head of Bucks CID, Malcolm Fewtrell, visits the farm at 1.30 pm, and tells the waiting media that:

"The whole place is one big clue." The media dub Leatherslade Farm, "Backnote Farm".

McArthur has been given a number of nicknames by his contacts, when checked they refer to John Daly, Gordon Goody, Roy James, Bruce Reynolds and Charlie Wilson.

A dress shop in Church Street in Reigate in Surrey becomes suspicious of a lady customer paying for a number of items with dirty £1 notes. The customer's husband, James Patten, is traced to 66 The Woodlands, Beulah in Croydon after the shop assistant notes down the customer's car registration number.

After talking to other shop owners in Church Street the police discover that the couple (Jimmy White and his wife) had given their address in other stores as Clovelly Caravan Site, Bexhill Road, Boxhill, Surrey, and given their name as Ballard. The caravan is searched and police find £136 in a jacket pocket, worth about £2,300 at 2013 values. They decide to put surveillance on the caravan.

Concerned about hearing no news of the farm being cleaned, Reynolds, Edwards, Wilson and James meet at a transport café on the North Circular Road at 2.30 pm. They plan to go to the farm to do the clean up themselves. Just before they leave for the farm at 4.30 pm they pick up a copy of the evening newspaper.

The London evening papers are reporting that the 'hideout' has been found. An incident room has been set up at Brill police station. The papers also mention that Tommy Butler, the Grey Fox, has been brought in to head up the investigation.

During the day the driver of the Midday Scot express involved in the Boxing Day disaster that killed 18 people, John Russell, admits to passing a red signal and is officially blamed for the collision. The train in question is the same one as the Great Train Robbery but nobody makes the link on that day.

1963 - Wednesday, 14 August
Bob Welch's house at 30A Benyon Road in Islington, London N12 is visited in the early hours by detectives

from Scotland Yard. Welch is not at home.

Police start a three-day examination of Leatherslade Farm. 243 photographs are taken of 311 fingerprints and 56 palm prints. Police also collect material left at farm. This includes mailbags and clothing as well as £541 in cash. There are also instructions for the use of the handcuffs, and famously a Monopoly set (which had the prints of Reynolds [2], Daly [8] and Biggs [1]), as well as Snakes & Ladders, Ludo and a chess set. Among the clothing were balaclavas, a Lieutenant's jacket with an SAS badge, and a Corporal's jacket with a Parachute regiment badge.

Fewtrell pays Brian Field a visit at his home.

John Daly, with his wife Barbara, and daughter Lorraine, book into the Endcliffe Hotel, First Avenue, Cliftonville in Kent as Mr and Mrs Cox-Daly.

Detective Sergeants Jack Slipper and Steve Moore visit 262 Fieldgate Mansions in Stepney, the home of Henry 'Harry' Smith and his wife Margaret Wade. They have a warrant to search for stolen bank notes. None are found. Smith is not at the flat but calls and speaks to Slipper. He promises to come and meet Slipper in the coming days.

The "Squealer" is reported by the media as having given Scotland Yard the names of 10 possible suspects. Millen and Hatherill say the names come from an informant they visited in prison.

The first arrest. Sergeant Stanley Davies and Constable Charles Case arrest Roger Cordrey and Bill Boal at 9 pm in Tweedale Road in Bournemouth. Cordrey and Boal have just finished putting Cordrey's share in a lock up that is owned by a police widow, Mrs Emily Clarke. Mrs Clarke, of 45 Tweedale Road, had become suspicious when Cordrey had offered three months rent in advance. She calls the police.

From the Austin van in the garage the police recover £56,047. Later in a garage at 59 Ensbury Avenue, another car is found in the boot of which are six bags containing another £79,892. Cordrey had hidden the key to this car in his rectum, but panicked at the station and asked to have a doctor remove it.

HOW IT HAPPENED—THE BIGGEST ROBBERY EVER

The actual engine at Cheddington Station

Bridego Bridge, 1963

SEARS CROSSING

Glove

HVP Carriage

Dead Phonebox

Track at Sears Crossing

Uncoupled

in for probe

IT MAY TOP £2,500,000!

ARMED GUARDS ON TRAINS?

Police guard at Cheddington

ROYAL MAIL

Inside the HVP carriage

WE'VE FOUND THE GANG'S HIDEOUT

Land Rover

Austin truck

Two Land Rovers, one number plate

Police discover Leatherslade Farm

Kitchen

Gang's radios

THE BANDITS' LARDER
WITH THE WOMAN'S TOUCH

Det Chief Sup Tommy Butler ('Grey Fox'), Det Sup Gerald McArthur, Det Sgt Jack Pritchard and Det Chief Supt Malcolm Fewtrell

Robbers' stores

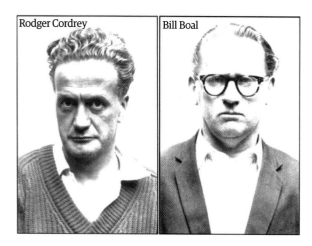

Rodger Cordrey

Bill Boal

Cordrey will plead guilty. He tells the police that he had been asked for his advice on how the train could be stopped and he had explained how to do it, saying, "I told them what to do about the signals." None of Cordrey (or Boal's) fingerprints were ever found at Leatherslade Farm.

1963 - Thursday, 15 August
At 3 am police find a briefcase containing £5,070 in the flat rented by Boal at 935 Wimborne Road and a pillowcase with £840. The total recovered by the police in Bournemouth stands at £141,017.

Bill Boal's wife, Rene, is arrested at 3.30 am in her house. She has £30 of train robbery money. Alfred and Mary Florence Pilgrim, Cordrey's sister and brother-in-law, are also arrested – in East Molsey, Surrey – for receiving (they were given £880 by Cordrey). The women are remanded to Holloway.

The media suggest that Billy Hill, one of the best-known London gangsters of the 1960s and a man who had been credited with the Eastcastle Street robbery, is the brain behind the Great Train Robbery. Tracked to Cannes, Hill denies it. Buster Edwards moves into Old Forge, Crescent in Shepperton.

1963 - Friday, 16 August
At 9 am three cases (a camel leather briefcase, a brown leather briefcase and a holdall) with money stacked inside them are found just off Coldharbour Lane in Dorking Woods in Surrey by John Ahern and Esa Hargreaves. The couple are on a motorbike that is overheating. Having stopped they see the bags lined up 20 yards off the road. When they discover the bags contain money they decide they must call the police. They flag a car down and ask the driver

to contact the police while they watch the bags. Detective Inspector Basil West attends the scene. Close by he finds a fourth bag, a suitcase, which is also full of money.

In one of the bags, the holdall, is a receipt for Herr e Frau Field from the Hotel Sonnenbichl in Bad Hindelang in Southern Germany. The Fields had stayed at the hotel for two weeks from 2 to 16 February 1963. In total the bags contain £100,900 (£1.7 million at 2013 rates).

In February 1965, Brian Field's father, Reginald Field, will make a statement to Tommy Butler that he found the bags in his garage at 141 Constance Road, Whitton, Middlesex. Field Sr said he got a friend of

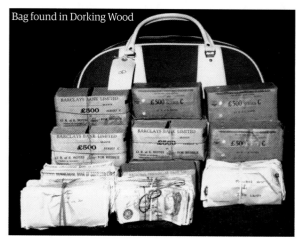

Bag found in Dorking Wood

his son, Gordon Neal, to drive him to the Dorking Woods on the night of 15 August where he disposed of the bags. The police always felt Brian Field was probably with them.

Bob Welch is finally questioned by the Flying Squad. He says that on 7 August he was at the Express Café in Elephant and Castle. Then visited a betting shop in Aldgate, before spending the evening at Wimbledon greyhound track.

Tommy Butler sends a list of 18 names of suspects to the Post Office Investigation Branch. The Flying Squad discovers that nine of the names on the list have cast-iron alibis, while one has already been dead for nine months.

The 18 suspects include Bruce Reynolds, Gordon Goody, Charlie Wilson, Jimmy White, Bobby Welch, Roy James and John Daly. Also on the list are the brothers Henry and Hayden Smith, Michael Kehoe,

Frederick Robinson, Jack Cramer, Charles Lilley, William Ambrose, Kenneth Shakeshaft, brothers Terry and George Sansom, and Harry Pitts, who had died in Parkhurst in November 1962.

1963 - Saturday, 17 August

Newspapers publish the famous photo of suspects covered in blankets as they are taken into Linslade Magistrates Court. This iconic photo does not actually include any major player from the train robbery, just people accused of receiving stolen money or helping Cordrey and Boal.

While watching television Reynolds sees pictures of his black Austin Healey and the news that the police are now looking for it. Reynolds drives it to a car park close to London airport and abandons it.

1963 - Sunday, 18 August

A man, Harry Browne, is stopped by police entering the caravan in Clovelly Caravan Park at Box Hill in Surrey. He is questioned and allowed to go. Once police are sure that Ballard and Patten are in fact Jimmy White, they do a more thorough inspection of the caravan and find £30,440 in cash from the train robbery hidden in the panelling.

Roy James wins his race at Cadwell Park.

1963 - Monday, 19 August

The Daily Express reports about the black Austin Healey bought by Mary Manson in Chiswick. A man, having seen the TV report, tells the police that he had seen it parked outside Walpole Lodge in Culmington Road, Ealing on 17 and 18 August.

On 18 August the police had visited Walpole Lane and discovered that Terry Hogan, a good friend of Bruce Reynolds, lived there.

The lorry and Land Rovers are moved from Leatherslade Farm to Aylesbury police station. The police also remove the number plates from the vehicles. Possessions from the kitchen, including food, are also removed from the farm.

An estate agent visits Buster Edwards' flat at 214 St Margarets Road, East Twickenham to discover the family has moved out.

1963 - 21 August

Terry Hogan is questioned by Scotland Yard and asked where he was on 7 and 8 August, Hogan explains he had been in Cannes.

Mary Manson, also known as Mrs Macdonald, who had been visiting John Daly in Kent, is visited at her house at 4 Wimbledon Close, The Downs, Wimbledon. She has just returned to London after visiting Daly in Kent. After a search of the house she is charged with receiving £833 in stolen money. This is linked to the purchase of the Austin Healey in Chiswick.

1963 - 22 August

Mary Manson appears in court and is represented by Wilfred Fordham. She is remanded to Holloway.
Charlie Wilson is arrested at his home at 45 Crescent Lane, Clapham, SW4 at 12.55 pm by Detective Sergeant Nigel Reid. The house is searched, but without a warrant. Wilson is taken to Cannon Row police station next to Scotland Yard and questioned by Butler. Wilson is the first major player in Reynolds' firm to be arrested.

Wilson's fingerprints have been found on the kitchen windowsill, Saxa salt drum, and the cellophane

METROPOLITAN POLICE

On the 8th August, 1963, the Glasgow to Euston mail train was robbed of about two and a half million pounds.

Substantial rewards will be paid to persons giving such information as will lead to the apprehension and conviction of the persons responsible.

The assistance of the public is sought to trace the whereabouts of the after described persons:

Persons having information are asked to telephone WHItehall 1212 or the nearest Police Station.

wrapping of a Johnson's First Aid Travel Kit. Wilson is taken to Aylesbury and charged. Charges for those arrested are made at Linslade Magistrate Court. Male prisoners are then moved to HMP Bedford and women to HMP Holloway.

Charlie Wilson arrested

Gordon Goody

Brian Field

Mug shots are circulated to the media for Reynolds, White and Wilson. White's wife, Sheree, and her dog 'Gigi' are also featured along with other wives. Director of Public Prosecutions is concerned that this may be considered prejudicial to a fair trial.
Police visit the racing garage of Roy James in Battersea. He is away testing at Goodwood. They seize James' Mini.

Reynolds, who has been house hunting in the Midlands with Freddie Foreman, rushes back to London as the garage where his and Daly's money from the robbery is stored, can be traced to him. He moves the money to a safe house.

Frances Reynolds has also seen the photos as she shops in Oxford Street and decides it is best not to return to the Queensway flat. She hides in a house in Canterbury for a week, not knowing if Bruce is safe.

Gordon Goody decides to pay a visit to Margaret Perkins, a 'beauty queen' ex-girlfriend from Leicester. His car breaks down en route, close to Bedford, and he arrives late in Leicester by hire car.

1963 - 23 August
Gordon Goody is arrested in room 202 at the Grand Hotel, Leicester after being mistaken for Bruce Reynolds by a florist who had delivered flowers to the room.

Goody has used glasses as a disguise. Dragged from his bed at 2 am he is held overnight. Perkins has her house searched later in the morning.

While Goody is in custody the police visit the Windmill Public House, 17 Upper Ground, London SE1 and ask the licensee if they can search his daughter's bedroom where they believe Goody had been staying.

At the end of the search they take away a pair of brown suede shoes, Trueform, size 10. With the police is Dr Ian Holden, a Scotland Yard forensic expert. A man who had been humiliated by Goody during the trial for the London airport job.

Roy James is now listed by police as a person of interest. He is given the nickname of 'The Weasel' by mistake, but the media picks up the name and it sticks.

Reynolds is now based in a friend's house in Wimbledon. He admits to drinking a bottle of vodka a day due to the stress. In North West Italy, a waiter tells police he is certain that one of three men he served on 22 August was Reynolds. It was not.

1963 - 24 August
Goody is taken to Aylesbury and interviewed by Butler at midnight and again at 1 am. At a third interview at 11.45 am Butler tells Goody that they now know he flew to Belfast on 2 August with his mother and another man, Knowles, but that he

returned alone on 6 August. So no alibi for Goody for 7 and 8 August.

Inspector Basil Morris and Sergeant Church visit Biggs at 6.45 pm at 37 Alpine Road in Redhill looking for Reynolds. Biggs says he has not seen him for some time. There is no suggestion that Biggs may be a suspect.

1963 - 25 August
The police guard on Leatherslade Farm is dropped. Goody is released at 12.15 am and not charged.

Butler in person drives him to his home in Putney. Butler tells his team to discover where Goody was between 6 and 9 August.

1963 - 26 August
Leatherslade Farm is handed back to its previous owner, Bernard Rixon.

Police search Bill Boal's house in Fulham. They take away a set of knuckledusters, a blue jacket and a cap.

Later the police will say that the yellow paint found on a watch winder in the right jacket pocket is of the same colour and chemical composition as will be found on Gordon Goody's shoes, and match the paint at Leatherslade Farm.

Following a tip off, Scotland Yard ask Interpol to look for Roy James in Vienna. Daly moves out of the Endcliffe Hotel in Cliftonville, Kent and returns to London

The Police Gazette carries a five-page special giving the numbers of the £5 notes known to have been stolen from the train. The numbers known are only a tiny fraction of the stolen money.

1963 - 27 August
A police informant gives Commander Hatherill a list of 14 suspects. They include Bruce Reynolds, Gordon Goody, Charlie Wilson, Buster Edwards, Jimmy White, Roger Cordrey, Bobby Welch, Roy James, John Daly, Thomas Wisbey, James Hussey and Brian Field. Also on the list are Henry Smith, Daniel Pembroke and two post office employees.

The police also investigate 35 GPO officers that could have had information about the contents of the train's HVP coach. Two Irishmen on the list receive special attention, Michael Lyttle from London and Thomas McCarthy from Glasgow. There were 16 Irishmen travelling on the actual train. Reynolds has moved to a small flat in Clapham.

1963 - 28 August
Rixon opens Leatherslade Farm up to the public. 50 people turn up to view the farm on the first day. The police will still take evidence from the farm even after the public has been through it

Sixteen days after finding the farm, and four days after the police guard is dropped, a tin of yellow paint is taken by the police from Leatherslade Farm. It is handed to Dr Holden on 29 August. Scotland Yard closes down its Great Train Robbery incident room. Since opening on 8 August it has received 1,651 messages.

Martin Luther King Jr delivers his "I Have a Dream" speech in Washington.

The Story that refuses to die.....

Popular culture and how legends are made

In understanding how the Great Train Robbery has become the UK's most iconic heist, one only has to look at the sheer volume of material, in numerous mediums, that it has spawned. As a cash cow, media capitalist constructed tales of the robbery have generated many millions more than the original sum stolen on the Glasgow-Euston Up Special.

There have been an immeasurable quantity of print in newspapers and books, and many hours of film from documentaries to movies based on or inspired by the Great Train Robbery of 1963. Except for Jack the Ripper, no crime (and certainly no single crime) has been the subject of so much coverage, defining an era in British history. The story of the robbery and the fate of the men who carried it out reads like a fantastic Hollywood script. A daring heist, police corruption, capture, record sentences, betrayal, escape, plastic surgery, Nazis, assassination, revenge, kidnapping and retribution.

From the moment the news broke up until today, not one year has passed without a mention of the robbery in the media.

By retelling and capitalising on these stories, the press, publishing houses and the entertainment industry have all inadvertently glamorised and created one of England's most enduring contemporary legends, deeply entrenching the robbers' deeds into British culture and folklore.

When news of the robbery was first released, it was reported as the Cheddington Mail Van Raid, but as details of the spectacular heist emerged, the media decided this name didn't quite live up to the scale of the crime and, always quick to sensationalise and maximise sales, looked for something more catchy thus "The Great Train Robbery" was born, or rather,

reborn, as that oddly grandiose title was in fact heisted from a popular and iconic American film of the same name, made 60 years previously.

American history is steeped in tales of train robbers, outlaws, and their exciting exploits whether in print or film, appealed strongly to the public of post-war Britain, with its voracious appetite for American culture at the time. Western films were particularly popular.

The adventures of lawless desperados and the relentless men who hunted them down made for exciting and gripping stories. In fact, Bruce Reynolds grew up on the exploits of Jesse James and Butch Cassidy and the Sundance Kid. Detective Superintendant Tommy Butler, head of the Flying Squad, and the robbers' nemesis, was an avid fan of Westerns and one of his only passions apart from his police job, was to watch them repeatedly.

Alluding further to this picaresque genre, some papers covering the robbery used a Western font complete with cartoon six guns and steam trains, evoking by association the robbery to the train robberies of the American Wild West.

Subsequently, just as the media in America had turned their train robbers into folkloric icons, the same was to happen in the UK.

The Great Train Robbery occurred during the wettest and coldest summer in living memory. In this bleak grey climate, the country was reeling in the scandalous wake of the Profumo Affair. John Profumo was the cabinet war minister, who was exposed for having sex with Christine Keeler, a vice girl, and mistress of a Soviet naval attaché and suspected KGB agent. The nation was flabbergasted and the government's reputation ruined.

Following the public outcry, the shocking revelations rocked the comfy certainties of the post war consensus, and ushered in, an edgy anti-establishment undercurrent. Amidst this groundswell of rebellion, the government was regarded as having been caught with its pants down, with the train robbers then giving the establishment a jolly good spanking. Cheers instead of condemnation prevailed with many toasting the robbers with 'the best of British luck to them'.

The initial media coverage of the robbery might have felt like a welcome distraction from the public outrage and fallout of the Profumo Affair, but before long it too became another thorn in the authorities' side, as the press gleefully used the robbery to embarrass them further. This only goaded the Establishment into overreaction, as by robbing the Royal Mail, the Queen's mail, they had thrown down the gauntlet, which the authorities were determined to pick up at any cost in order to save face, with a vengeance.

As the judge passed out the sentences there were gasps of disbelief in the court and all over the country. The unprecedented sentences induced public sympathy. The British tradition of rooting for the underdog prevailed, with the robbers, perceived as rebels, unfairly punished for kicking back at an out of touch elitist corrupt system. This attitude would ultimately lead to the convicted to be perversely viewed as modern-day Robin Hoods.

When the words: They've stolen a train!... hit the airwaves, the nation was staggered and excited by the audacity of the heist and the amount of money stolen, as estimated figures escalated to the final £2.6 million, (worth about £46 million today) and weighing around 2½ tons. Immediately a media frenzy ensued, even across the Atlantic. The New York Herald Tribune fuelled the hype with, *World's greatest robbery. There will always be an England!* blazoned across its front page. They also commented, 'Although the train robbery is likely to be associated with America's Wild West, this fell deed has a peculiarly British quality. Perhaps because of a long tradition of highly literate writers on sophisticated crime, British criminals tend to avoid the blood and thunder style of the James boys and do their work with exceptional finesse'.

The normally serious New York Times expressed the hope that the 'imperturbable James Bond be put on the case' and added 'undoubtedly Goldfinger or Dr No is behind this incredibly efficient bit of larceny'.

Soon the press was asking who could be capable of such an operation, as it didn't seem possible that any ordinary, organised criminals could have undertaken it. The robbery appeared to have been carried out with slickness and military precision. Reports that the gang wore army outfits and used army vehicles with the leader (Reynolds) wearing the uniform of an SAS Major, led to much wild speculation, creating

NEWS OF THE WORLD

SUNDAY, AUGUST 18, 1963   EMPIRE NEWS   No. 6,249   PRICE SIXPENCE

HUNT ON FOR THE COMMANDO MAJOR

fantastic headlines such as *Hunt for Commando Major* and *Balaclava and the 40 Thieves*.

The notion that The Major, or whomever he was working for, was a criminal mastermind, soon became implanted. The robbery became the topic of the moment and the press were having a field day with avid readers eager to catch up on daily events as they unfolded. Only five days after the robbery, the hideout at Leatherslade Farm was discovered and quickly dubbed 'Robbers' Roost' by the media, another nod to the Wild West and the legendary hideout of the infamous, Hole in the Wall gang.

'Great Train Robbery, hows that going?'

The evidence apparently found there, confirmed names already given to the police via informants. Soon there were many arrests, leading to the longest trial in British history, ending with sentences totalling 307 years between them.

Just eleven days before the verdict, The Beatles had

sensationally made history in Billboard's 'Hot 100' by occupying the first five slots in the charts. Whilst the world's focus and fascination turned to Britain, the robbers made history again with the enormity of their record breaking punishment. To many onlookers, this band of young men surprisingly did not look like stereotypical criminals. Like The Beatles, they appeared as cheeky chappies, attractive, stylish, and well groomed, and both as working class groups who had hit the big time. Despite fortunes made on different sides of the tracks, the Fab 4 and the Great Train Robbers were regarded across the globe as iconic ambassadors of the new British Quintessential cool.

The sentences became a subject of fierce debate, fuelling public outrage, with many saying they were far too long, compounding sympathy for the robbers. This sentiment was obviously already on the mind of the Judge

Edmund Davies, when he made his summing-up statement prior to sentencing, 'let us clear out of the way any romantic notions of daredevilry...'

Then incredibly, much to the nation's amazement, Charlie Wilson and Ronnie Biggs both made spectacular prison escapes, from supposedly inescapable prisons. Wilson from HMP Winson Green, considered to be the British Alcatraz, and Biggs from 'The Hate Factory' HMP Wandsworth. Once again the robbers had defiantly cocked a snook to the powers that be, heightening the drama and the public's delight. The author Graham Greene wrote to the Daily Telegraph asking:

'Am I one of a minority in feeling admiration for the skill and courage behind The Great Train Robbery? More important, am I in a minority in being shocked by the savagery of the sentences? Thirty years for a successful theft, as compared with a life sentence, (twelve years at most in practice) for the rape and murder of a child. If our legal system sentences a man to thirty years for an offence against property, it is not surprising if some of us feel sympathy for the prisoner who escapes, again with skill and courage from such a sentence?'

That evening it was evident that Greene was not a minority when TV interviewers asked the public would they disclose Wilson's whereabouts if they knew them. The almost unanimous reply was 'No'.

Wilson and Biggs,
Madame Tussauds

The establishment's hard line had backfired, shooting themselves in the foot. They had alienated themselves further, from the man on the street and the legacy of the draconian sentences was to inadvertently create the rise of gun culture in the UK. Life in 1963, for killing someone with a gun was 25 years, but the train robbers, who only had coshes and pickaxe handles, (contrary to popular belief, they were not for deliberately hitting people, but to break into the HVP and intimidate the workers) got a whopping thirty. The message to future robbers was clear; you might as well carry a gun.

Other foiled escape attempts, and prison protests against the high levels of security were reported in the media and the robbers were eventually moved to a purpose-built special secure unit at maximum-security prison HMP Parkhurst on the Isle of Wight.

At the time it was outlandishly claimed by Chief Constable of Durham Alec Muir that there was a real danger that the robbers would be released from jail with the use of tanks, bombs and atomic weapons. He further added that it was immoral that someone should be locked away for 30 years, and that it would be more humane to eliminate the robbers than have them serve such long sentences. In Goody's case he said, 'I would be prepared to shoot Mr Goody quietly more than I would be prepared to shoot an enemy in war.'

Meanwhile, everyone was asking, 'Where is the loot?' Only £280,000 has been recouped, less than a tenth of the total stolen. The enormous and unprecedented reward offering £260,000 for information, created an army of amateur sleuths. Then £101,000 was found left in a Dorking wood and another £30,440 was discovered in a caravan 8 miles away. A further £47,000 was found left in a telephone box. Soon people all over the country, attracted by the lure of finding hastily abandoned cash, found themselves engaged in a feverous, national treasure hunt.

Also, Reynolds, White and Edwards were still on the run with constant speculation on their whereabouts. Recent escapees Charlie Wilson and Ronnie Biggs were both immortalised as wax figures for Madame Tussaud's.

As the saga continued, the public fervently followed the progress of determined Detective Superintendant Tommy Butler in his personal quest to track them down in a classic cops-and robbers tale. Spurning retirement it took him 5 years to finally catch the robbers, Reynolds being the last - all except for Biggs.

In 1978, with Reynolds and Wilson still behind bars, the train robbers were back in the limelight collaborating with author Piers Paul Read for his book **The Train Robbers.** The gang fantastically claimed the robbery had been sponsored by none other than, L Col. Otto Skorzeny; once Hitler's favourite poster boy commando rescuer of Mussolini, founder of ODESSA and holder of The Iron Cross. However when Read flew to Brazil, he was told that it was all a hoax by Biggs.

Biggs' own story was to add another incredible dimension escaping from the UK and Australia, countless girls in Rio a pop-star son, a mercenary kidnapping and a failed extradition. Biggs became a Brazilian celebrity and tourist attraction and sellable worldwide media fodder. Promoted by the press, he became an embodiment of the loveable, lucky rogue living the high life, beyond the reach of the law - a British flag in one hand, a V sign in the other

Shoot the Train Gang, says Muir

IT would be more humane to shoot the Great Train Robbers than to lock them up, said the Chief Constable of County Durham, Mr. Alec Muir, last night.

This image was to resonate strongly back in the UK, especially in the late 70's when a disenfranchised youth embraced the nihilism of Punk Rock.

Adding further to Biggs' cultural status, he was inaugurated as a singer/songwriter with the infamous punk band the Sex Pistols, reinforcing the concept, to a new generation, that the train robbery was an act of anarchy.

After running for 37 years Biggs returned to the UK in a private jet, with his son Michael, Bruce Reynolds and his son Nick, courtesy of the Sun newspaper. His larger than life exploits and adventures had entertained the public and kept the legend alive, further aggravating the establishment for four decades. Ex-police commissioner Sir Robert Marks was to comment 'Biggs added a rare and welcome touch of humour to the history of crime'.

And the story doesn't end there.

In the interim many other compelling episodes have kept the story alive and on the front pages. Incidents like the shocking assassination of Charlie Wilson and subsequent retributions; Wisbey and Hussey convicted for drug charges; Roy James shooting his father-in-law; the puzzling suicide of Buster Edwards; and Ronnie Biggs return and release have all contributed to keeping the book open on this subjec that has essentially become a unique 50-year media crimina soap opera.

As the robbery celebrates its 50th anniversary, of the 16 men who were at the track only Goody, Welch, Wisbey and Biggs are still alive. In February 2013 Bruce Reynolds died aged 81, followed weeks later by his brother in law, John Daly, aged 82 More documentaries are in the works and the BBC is producing two 90-minute films based or the robbery, following ITV's previous success with *Mrs Biggs* - all further adding to its legacy and securing The Great Train Robbery as Britain's most iconic and famous crime.

Ronnie Biggs & Steve Jones recording *No One is Innocent*

BUCKINGHAMSHIRE CONSTABULARY

£10,000 REWARD

ROBBERY

About 3 a.m. 8th August, 1963 from the Glasgow—Euston mail train

REGISTERED PACKETS

The above reward will be paid by the Postmaster General to the first person giving such information as will lead to the apprehension and conviction of the persons responsible for this robbery.

Information to be given to the Chief Constable, Buckinghamshire Constabulary, Aylesbury (Tel.: AYLESBURY 5010), or at any Police Station.

PART THREE

AFTERMATH OF THE ROBBERY:
Trials and Tribulations - no one is innocent

1963 - 30 August
Frances Reynolds is recognised in the local butcher she is using. John Daly, who is married to France's sister, is listed by Scotland Yard as a man they want to talk to along with his wife Barbara. Images of the Bruce, Frances, John and Barbara are shown on the evening news.

Bob Welch moves into the Harbour Light Hotel in Mevagissey.

1963 - 2 September
Reynolds moves in to a flat in Handcroft Road, Thornton Heath in Croydon. It is above a cleaner.

Ronnie Biggs

James Hussey

1963 - 4 September
Ronald Biggs is arrested at 6.20 pm at 37 Alpine Road in Redhill by Detective Inspector Frank Williams. He is taken to Scotland Yard at 7.30 pm where Butler questions him. Biggs refuses to sign a statement. He is transferred to Aylesbury. Police find Biggs' fingerprints on a blue-edged Pyrex plate and a bottle of ketchup. He is the ninth person arrested in relation to the robbery.

1963 - 5 September
Biggs is formally charged at Linslade Magistrates Court and sent to HMP Bedford. Another person arrested and charged on this day is Christine Keeler,

a key figure in the Profumo Affair. On 6 December she will be sentenced to 9 months in prison.

1963 - 6 September
Scotland Yard is tipped off about a possible attempt to rob the Weymouth to London, via Woking, service. The West Travelling Post Office Night Up. En route the train picks up surplus money from the banks. Woking or Weybridge are the expected site of the robbery.

The police take a closer look at the threat in December 1963 when they believe the job is being planned for the Christmas holidays or early 1964. This is the same train Reynolds had looked at in early 1963, and by January 1964 the police still believe Reynolds is planning another train robbery.

1963 - 7 September
Jimmy Hussey is arrested at 8 Edridge House, Dog Kennel Hill, London SE22. The evidence is a palm print on the Austin lorry. Police also visit the home of Tommy Wisbey at 27 Ayton House, Elmington Estate in Camberwell. He is not there, but they speak to his wife Rene. Rene says Tommy has run off to Spain with another woman. Another suspect, Daniel Pembroke, also lives on the estate.

1963 - 8 September
Bob Welch checks out of the Harbour Light Hotel in Mevagissey and moves to the Headland Hotel in Newquay.

1963 - 9 September
Roger Cooke, the Conservative MP for Twickenham, criticises the people of Oakley for not catching and stopping the gang when they were at Leatherslade Farm.

1963 - 10 September
The head of the Flying Squad, Ernie Millen, is

promoted to Deputy Commander at New Scotland Yard reporting to George Hatherill. The new head of the Flying Squad is Tommy Butler, the Grey Fox.

1963 - 11 September

Tommy Wisbey calls Scotland Yard and agrees to meet Frank William at 11.30 am at his betting shop at 1 Redcross Way, London SE1. The shop is jointly owned with Freddie Foreman and William Gorbell. He is taken to Scotland Yard. Evidence is his fingerprints on an attachment to the bath. Harry Smith is also arrested but is let go after being interviewed by Butler. There is no evidence against him.

Tommy Wisbey

Leonard Field

1963 - 13 September

After the publication of a photo of Buster Edwards and his wife, a lady calls the police to say that their neighbours at Old Forge Crescent in Shepperton, Mr & Mrs Green, look very like them. The police visit the house but they miss Edwards by a matter of hours. He has left in a Morris 1100 that is found abandoned in Ealing. The theory is that a policeman tipped Edwards off. Edwards moves the family a short distance to Sunnymead, a house in Wraysbury, Buckinghamshire that backs on to River Thames.

1963 - 14 September

Leonard Field is arrested at 262 Green Lane, Harringay, London N4, as the purchaser of Leatherslade Farm. Field asks that John Wheater be called in to represent him. Both men are kept apart by Scotland Yard to make statements over the purchase of Leatherslade Farm.

1963 - 15 September

Fewtrell visits Brian Field and over a cup of tea gets him to admit that a German hotel bill is his. Fewtrell had found it in the bag in Dorking Woods with over £100,000 of train robbery money. Field is arrested, taken to Scotland Yard and charged.

1963 - 16 September

"Anyone who acquired Leatherslade Farm and remained in possession and control during the relevant period, in default of a water tight explanation, must be an accessory to the robbery," says Detective Chief Inspector Mesher of the Fraud Squad. Brian and Leonard Field are transferred to Aylesbury Police Station.

1963 - 17 September

Bob Welch, Daniel Pembroke, Ronald Harvey, John Sturm and Charles Lilly, are all considered suspects for one reason or another, and are spotted in and around Beaford in Dorset, staying at Beaford House.

Detective Chief Inspector Frank Williams believes the men are carrying train robbery money to hide.

1963 - 19 September

Over a month since finding Leatherslade Farm, Detective Constable Keith Milner finds yellow paint on the clutch and break pedal of a Land Rover from the farm, plus some khaki paint.

1963 - 26 September

Preliminary hearing and the committal proceedings take place for the people charged. The court will sit for 19 days between 26 September and 2 December. Mary Manson is finally released on bail.

1963 - 28 September

Dr Ian Holden visits Leatherslade Farm to examine the garage and take further paint samples.

1963 - 30 September

Charles Connelly, who took part in an armed robbery of the Royal Arsenal Co-operative Society depot in Mitcham Surrey on 17 November 1962, during which a driver was shot and killed, has his sentence reduced to ten years from 15 years by a court of appeal. The judge notes: "Gravely reprehensible as his conduct was this court is of the opinion that the sentence was excessive and should be reduced to ten years."

The judge is Mr Justice Edmund Davies who in six months time will decide that a sentence of 30 years for a crime where there was no loss of life is in no way excessive.

1963 - 1 October
Matin Harvey, a brother of an associate of Bob Welch, is arrested at 17 Michaelson House, Bowen Drive, London SE21. £518 in £1 notes is found in the house. Having pleaded guilty, he will be sentenced to 12 month for receiving on 17 April 1964.

1963 - 3 October
Goody is re-arrested and taken to Putney police station. At 2.50 pm he is interviewed and shown the shoes that will be used as the evidence to charge him. He readily admits that the shoes are his as he knows they were never anywhere near the Leatherslade Farm. With Goody arrested and charged, Tommy Butler is now looking for Bruce Reynolds, Buster Edwards, Jimmy White, John Daly, Roy James and Bob Welch.

1963 - 10 October
A man called Walter Smith is arrested at 14 Linel House, Murray Grove, Shoreditch N1 and charged with receiving £2,000 of train robbery money. Patricia Smith is also charged as her knickers are stuffed with money (£470). The couple were drying the money that had got wet in their roof.

It is later discovered by the police that Smith was laundering the money by buying £5 postal orders. Police believe the money was from Harry Smith's share of the train robbery, but still have no evidence to charge him.

Police take possession of Roy James' Brabham Ford, Formula Junior racing car from a garage in Spicer Street, London SW11. The fact that James' never calls about it or his Mini is seen as an admission of guilt.

Brian Field is given permission to leave Aylesbury Prison to visit his wife at home. Karin has given birth to their daughter four months prematurely. The baby had been removed to Battle Hospital in Reading. The baby girl, Jacqueline, does not survive and is buried on 16 October when Field is allowed to attend the funeral.

John Daly and his wife move in to 65A Eaton Square in London SW1.

1963 - 14 October
Jack Mills is given a 25 guineas cheque from British Railways plus a certificate for "courage and resource".

1963 - 17 October
John Wheater is arrested at 7.40 am at 60 Ottways Lane, Ashstead in Surrey by Detective Chief Inspector Mesher.

1963 - 19 October
Alec Douglas-Home takes over as Prime Minister from Harold Macmillan who has resigned on the grounds of ill health.

1963 - 25 October
Bob Welch travels from Exeter to London to meet his brother at London Bridge railway station. He is arrested by Frank Williams as he walks to a car in Railway Approach, London SE1. He is taken to Scotland Yard and interviewed by Butler. The evidence is a palm print found on a pipkin of ale left in a cupboard in the farm. The can is one of the very few items from the Great Train Robbery to be found in Scotland Yard's own crime museum.

1963 - 26 October
Bob Welch is charged in Aylesbury.

1963 - Early November
Reynolds is taken to meet with John Daly, who is being hidden in a flat in Bryanston Square, close to Marble Arch. Daly wants to get control of his share of the money as he has plans for what he wants to

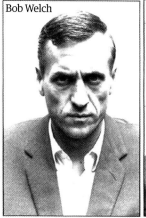
Bob Welch

John Weater

do with it with Michael Black and Bill Goodwin. Against his advice, Reynolds will arrange to have Daly's share dropped at the flat.

1963 - 4 November
The police look for Harry Smith at 496 Barking Road in Plaistow. The house is searched and £93 in £1 notes is found on Mrs Wade, Smith's wife.

1963 - 7 November
James Kensit (Jimmy the Dip), who was part of Bob Welch's alibi, calls Scotland Yard to say he won't back it up. Kensit was a known associate of the Krays and Richardsons. He is the father of the actress Patsy Kensit.

1963 - 8 November
Daly and William Goodwin drive to the village of St Juliot, near Boscastle, where Goodwin's mother and niece live in a house called Endelstowe. Here they bury £100,000 in the garden.

1963 - 10 November
Daly and Goodwin are involved in car accident in Old Northcott when they collide with cattle. Daly claims to the police to be Michael Black.

1963 - 22 November
The assassination of President John F. Kennedy takes place in Dallas, Texas. His assassin, Lee Harvey Oswald, is shot and killed two days later while in police custody.

1963 - 23 November
The BBC broadcasts the first episode of *Dr Who*.

1963 - Late November
Because of concerns about the Croydon flat, Reynolds moves to a friend's house close to Clapham Common. Goody, Wilson and Biggs look at various options to escape from HMP Bedford.

1963 - 2 December
All the prisoners arrested to date appear before Linslade Magistrates, sitting in Aylesbury, and the prosecution makes the case for them to be committed for trial. Charges against Mary Manson are dropped. The prosecution says that while they are convinced she went to the car showroom with

Bruce Reynolds, that does not then mean that the money she used was stolen. Manson receives costs.

All defence counsels make an argument that for a fair trial the case should be committed to the Old Bailey, the Central Criminal Court. This is rejected by the judge, as are all applications for bail. A request to move the prisoners to Brixton Prison is also turned down.

1963 - 3 December
At 4.15 pm John Daly is arrested at 65A Eaton Square in Belgravia by Tommy Butler and Frank Williams. Having observed the flat they know there is a secret ring (two short rings followed by one longer ring). Daly's wife Barbara opens the door and the police pile in. Daly is arrested in his pyjamas and a red dressing gown. He is taken to Scotland Yard.

Jon Daly

Living in Eaton Square Daly had been dressing the part of a city gent in bowler hat, city suit and had grown a prodigious black beard. His fingerprints had been found on the Monopoly board. In the flat in Eaton Square documents are found belonging to Michael Black. During the search William Goodwin walks in and is arrested for helping Daly. Daly is taken to Aylesbury and charged.

On news of Daly's arrest, Michael Black goes to Endelstowe in Cornwall and digs up part of Daly's money.

Police by chance visit the house in Clapham where Bruce and Frances Reynolds are hiding. They had spotted a ladder up against a first floor window. Frances opens door in a dressing gown, but Bruce has the presence of mind, despite drinking heavily because of the news of Daly, to take off all his clothes and play the part of a cheating lover. They are not recognised and an embarrassed police officer leaves. Only later do they recognise Bruce from a poster. Reynolds knows they will need to move on again quickly. By the time they returned, Reynolds had already moved on again.

When the police do discover the house, they also find the fingerprints of Daly and James.

Reynolds discovers that there has actually been a burglary in the house and a briefcase with £5,000 (about £86,000 in 2013 values) and jewellery has been stolen.

1963 - 4 December
Reynolds visits and buys a flat at 18 Albert Mews off the Gloucester Road. Bruce and Frances move in, it is their first real home in the four months since the robbery. Bruce will stay put and not leave the flat for six months. Terry Hogan visits and has a weekly delivery organised from a Jermyn Street wine merchant of one case of Nuits St. Georges, one case of Veuve Clicqout Rose and one case of Dom Perignon '55. Reynolds and his wife are desperate to see Nick, but it is too dangerous. Reynolds weight balloons from 13 1/2 stone to 16 stone. The flat has a phone, but no calls are made, just received.

1963 - 7 December
A female informant tells Scotland Yard that Roy James is living at 14 Ryder's Terrace, St John's Wood, London NW8, close to Abbey Road. She says he has boasted of an escape route. She also tells them he has grown a beard. Police check possible escape routes from the flat, including plans of the sewers. They find that the ground behind the house has been cleared to make a soft landing place for a possible jump from the roof.

1963 - 10 December
Police receive an anonymous message: "Go to the phonebox in Great Dover Street, opposite Blackhorse Court. You will find £50,000 in two sacks."

At around 6.35 pm, Butler and Williams find the money in the phonebox in old one pound notes and bundles of Scottish five pound notes. Scottish notes can be traced to money on the train. The total in the sacks is £47,245 (over £800,000 at 2013 values).

It is believed that the anonymous caller could have been linked to Frank Williams who had been contacted by Freddie Foreman about the drop. Foreman has discussed with Williams, who he trusts, that the police will not keep chasing a certain suspect or suspects in return for the cash.

Foreman first tried to hand the £50,000 to Williams at Nunhead Police station, close to one of Foreman's betting shops in Nunhead Lane. Foreman says William said he could not take it as Butler had backed out of the deal.

The second attempt at Great Dover Street is a location that Foreman can have watched from a flat belonging to his brother in law. A separate bundle of £10,000 was left on top to be dropped off at Albert Connell's betting shop. But Butler takes the lot to Scotland Yard. According to Foreman, the police following the drop, did not bother the suspect who was mentioned to Williams again.

Roy James

On the same day, Roy James is tracked to his mews flat at 14 Ryders Terrace in St Johns Wood and arrested after a spectacular roof top chase. The police have to break into the property and see James going out on the roof through a fanlight window. They are waiting for him at the drop spot.

James has £12,041 in his possession plus a scrap of paper with a figure of £109,500 on it. James is taken to Scotland Yard and interviewed by Butler.

Evidence is James' prints on a blue-glass Pyrex plate and a Johnson's First Aid Travel Kit that also had Charlie Wilson's prints on it. James' prints are also found on an American Magazine called Movie Screen. James becomes the third robber in two months to be found thanks to informants.

Cash left in phone box

1963 - 11 December

Money from the Great Dover Street drop is delivered to Aylesbury. Malcolm Fewtrell is surprised that the Flying Squad knew it was £50,000 as the Yard's only money counting machine has burnt out. Fewtrell finds the money is still damp and musty, suggesting it had been buried. It takes Fewtrell's team two full days to re-count the money as many notes are stuck together. His total is also £47,245.

1963 - December

Buster Edwards tries to cut a deal with the police. Freddie Foreman acts as the go between with Frank Williams.

Butler tells the media that he has 19 people in custody and is ready to start the court case. 12 have been charged with robbery (this includes Boal), eight charged with receiving stolen money, and one (Wheater) charged with conspiracy. However, less than 14% of the stolen money (£350,000) has been recovered.

The police are now certain of the involvement of Reynolds, Buster Edwards and Jimmy White, who are still on the run. Harry Smith and Daniel Pembroke are also considered strong suspects, while lesser suspects included Terry Hogan and Ronald Harvey.

George Stanley (Sturley), Biggs' solicitor, confirms to Wilson and Biggs that the main evidence against them, and the rest of the gang, will be fingerprints left at the farm. Stanley tells Wilson and Biggs to come up with a good reason as to why they would have visited the farm.

Edwards leaves England for Antwerp. He moves on to Cologne. Plastic surgery is organised by a contact of Freddie Foreman, Austrian born Ottto Skorzeny who had been a top ranking Nazi officer in the Waffen SS. Edwards will use Skorzeny as a massive red herring for Pierce Paul Read's book, 'The Train Robbers'. Edwards thought the story of Nazi involvement would get them a better advance for the book and take the spotlight off other people.

Jimmy White flees to Tangier.

Nine of the 16 members of the gang at the track are now in custody. [Wilson, Goody, James, Daly, Biggs, Cordrey, Wisbey, Welch, Hussey] The gang members are transferred from HMP Bedford to the hospital wing of HMP Aylesbury for the trial to begin. Experienced warders are brought in to babysit and look after the gang.

Goody, Wilson and Biggs now work on an escape plan, as the hospital wing is not as secure as a normal prison. First consideration is to dope the guards, but as the possible sentence (if convicted) is 15 years, they drop the idea. Instead a false key is organised through 'Johnny-the-Bosh' and everything is in place for a mass escape that nearly comes off.

Wilson's contacts are to leave a car at a spot near the back of the hospital. Boal will quietly cut the lock from the dormitory door in which he is held and which is less secure than the other cells. Once out he will unlock Goody's cell, which is next-door to the dormitory, with the false key. Goody will then unlock Wilson - who is on the same landing

Robbers arrive for court

- and they will take out the night watchman. They will then go down to the cells in the basement and unlock Biggs. On the night Boal loses his nerve and confesses the following day to the chief warder. All the privileges are withdrawn from the prisoners – and that includes having food and other luxuries brought in. Items discovered to have been smuggled in are confiscated.

1963 - 31 December
Committal proceeding for Roy James and John Daly at a special sitting of Linslade Magistrates at Leighton Buzzard.

1964 - 3 January
A 5-ton motor yacht named Christine is reported missing in the Channel after sailing from Ramsgate. Edward Anderson, who the police believe is an associate of Buster Edwards, owns the yacht. The only remains found of the yacht is an empty rubber dinghy tied to a buoy seven miles northeast of Broadstairs in Kent.

Daily Express reporters track Anderson, who is assumed dead, to Dublin. He says Dennis Bassett was in charge of the boat with two men. Bassett's body washes up in Belgium on 12 February. On 1 March The People runs a story quoting Anderson that the boat was carrying two train robbers and £1 million in bank notes. The police are not convinced by story, and decide it is a decoy set up by Buster Edwards to distract them.

1964 - 8 January
Beyond the Fringe introduces the sketch 'The Great Train Robbery' in to their Broadway show. In the sketch Alan Bennett interviews Peter Cook, who is playing the pompous deputy head of New Scotland Yard, Sir Arthur Gappy. Later in the year, the revue was finally recorded at the Shepherds Bush Empire for the BBC. The recording was thought to have been lost, and is only found in the Museum of Television and Radio in March 2005.

1964 - 20 January
Opening of the Great Train Robbery trial at the Buckingham Winter Assizes at the District Council Chamber in Aylesbury. Charges are mainly 'conspiracy to stop a mail with intent to rob said mail'. The accused are placed in a specially constructed dock. There are seats for sixty people in the public gallery.

Forty counsel, including 12 QCs are involved. Arthur James QC leads the prosecution. The 12-man jury is made up entirely of men. The judge is Mr Justice Edmund Davies.

Every morning, afternoon and evening the accused are locked into small individual compartments in a police bus, commonly known as a Black Maria. Then with an escort of at least four police cars and a dozen or so motorcycle police, they make the ten-minute journey to-and-from the prison and council chamber.

Caught "bang to rights", Cordrey pleads guilty at 10.27 am on the first day of the trial to conspiracy to stop the mail and receiving large sums of money from the robbery. He pleads not guilty to robbery with aggravation. The court accepts his plea and he is returned to prison to await sentencing.

Karin Field, the wife of Brian Field, is asked to address the court and explains that she was approached outside Reading Station by a man asking for £3,000 (about £50,000 in 2013 rates) to fix the jury. She informs the police who follow and arrest the man. He says he is acting for a third party. Butler releases the man saying he was simply an *agent provocateur*.

Wilson tells his wife to meet another would be extortionist at a house in Clapham. The extortionist is met by friends of Wilson who attempt to nail him to tree on Clapham Common. He escapes, but the wives are not bothered again.

The prosecution presents fingerprint evidence.

1964 - 22 January
Jack Mills is the first of 264 witnesses to give evidence. He is allowed to give his evidence from a chair. He is unable to identify any of the robbers.

The jury is taken to visit Leatherslade Farm.

1964 - 28 January
Gordon Goody's defence team successfully argue that as Goody had not been cautioned, all statements made by him between 23 August, when he was arrested in Leicester, to leaving Aylesbury police station on 25 August, must be inadmissible. There is also a reprimand from the judge to the police over searches made without the correct warrants.

1964 - 6 February
A retrial of Biggs - the Odd Man Out - is ordered after Detective Inspector Basil Morris lets slip in court that Biggs has served time in prison with Bruce Reynolds. The judge is not happy about the slip-up, and lets the police know.

1964 - 11 February
The prosecution rests. The prosecution case is clear

in that it is arguing that while it can't prove who was at the track and at the actual crime scene, if it proves somebody was at Leatherslade Farm that should be sufficient to prove the guilt of robbing Frank Dewhurst who was in charge of the HVP coach. The defence begins.

1964 - 12 February
Wisbey and Welch's defence teams start by arguing that their clients have no case to answer as there is no evidence to show when the prints had been left at the farm. If they had been left after 8 August they were not guilty of the charges against them. Hussey and Daly's defence also argue that there is not sufficient evidence against their clients to continue. Most of the charged make similar arguments in favour of no case to answer, with defence counsels questioning how the fingerprint evidence proves if and when the people were at Leatherslade Farm.

Justice Edmund Davies

1964 - 14 February
Mr Justice Edmund Davies gives his judgements on all defence submissions. It had been assumed all would be rejected but the judge surprises the court by saying that he will be directing the jury to acquit John Daly. Biggs, Hussey, James and Welch's submissions had been very similar to Daly's, but have been rejected.

Daly leaves the court a free man having spent 79 days in custody. A celebration party is organised for him by Mary Manson.

The accused are all still confident that they all have a reasonable explanation as to why their finger and palm prints were found at the farm. The defence arguments may have worked in individual cases, but with everyone coming up with different stories it does considerable harm to the credibility of any of the alibis.

1964 - 16 February

Bill Boal tells the court that he was beaten up by the police on his arrest. He also adds that he has never been to Leatherslade Farm or the "train spot".

He further argues that he only met up with Roger Cordrey because Cordrey owed him money and he needed it.

1964 - 17 February

Welch, Wisbey and Hussey try a joint defence argument that involves all their activities together to explain their prints being at the farm and on other items.

1964 - 19 February

Roy James starts his defence by presenting an alibi that he was never near the farm on the dates of the robbery. A witness statement puts Roy James on the Wescott Brill Road on 8 August, but the prosecution who have dismantled James' alibi does not use it.

1964 - 20 February

The defence for Gordon Goody begins. Goody still contends that he was in Ireland at the time of the robbery. The judge is not happy that by Goody arguing there was no paint on his shoes, he is suggesting that the police planted the paint

1964 - 21 February

First £10 notes in circulation since the Second World War.

1964 - 24 February

The defence for Brian Field begins. His counsel agrees that the bags in Dorking Woods belong to Field, but they argue that he did not put them there.

They also explain that the bags went missing from Field's office before the robbery. A witness to back up the story of the theft of the bags from the office is Field's first wife, Brenda, who still works at the company.

1964 - 28 February

The defence for John Wheater begins. A lot of his defence is simply based on his good character and witnesses that can attest for him. These include politicians and members of the armed forces.

1964 - 6 March

Expert evidence is given on Goody's behalf about the paint on his shoes. His expert says the paint in the Land Rover and on the shoes is not one and the same. Plus Goody never drove the Land Rovers.

John Maris, who had reported Leatherslade Farm to the police, is recalled to rebuff the defence of Hussey, Welch and Wisbey that a convoy of vehicles had arrived at the farm on 10 August.

1964 - 9 March

The arguments for the defence and prosecution come to an end. It is the 36th day of the trial. The crown says it will drop the charge of aggravated robbery against Brian Field.

Michael Black, who has stolen half of Daly's money, dies in London of an apparent heart attack.

1964 - 17-23 March

Summing up by Justice Edmund Davies. Some consider his 33-hour summing up a *tour de force*.

1964 - 23 March

The jury retires after a 49-day trial and at 4.52 pm are taken to a secret hide out (The Grange Youth Club, Wendover Way, Aylesbury) where they are kept, cut off from the outside world, until they reach their verdict.

After 66 hours in confinement – the longest in British legal history – the jury reach a verdict.

1964 - 26 March

At 10.30 am the jury return to the court. Guilty verdicts are handed down on the entire gang; the exception is the not guilty verdict for Brian Field on aggravated robbery or of receiving. Wheater is found not guilty of conspiracy. Each man stands, receives his verdict, and is then taken out by a prison officer.

The trial ends.

Daily Mirror

'Maximum security' at Aylesbury Jail

3d.   Thursday, April 16, 1964   No. 18,761

BRITAIN'S 12 MOST GUARDED MEN

Robert Welch | Roger Cordery | William Boal | Leonard Field | John Wheater | Charles Wilson | Roy James | James Hussey | Thomas Wisbey | Ronald Biggs | Brian Field | Douglas Goody

1964 - 30 March

Violent clash between Mods and Rockers at Clacton beach.

1964 - 8 April

Opening of Biggs' retrial at the Buckinghamshire Assizes, held in the Crown Court of Aylesbury.

1964 - 10 April

The prosecution, having made the same arguments as in the first case, but in a shorter form, rest. Biggs' defence explains that Biggs did visit Leatherslade Farm, but on 6 and 7 August, and to make a delivery and build a whipping post for a kinky party.

Biggs' defence team has not been told that two of the items Biggs' fingerprints have been found on (the Pyrex plate and bottle of ketchup) had been left by the owner of the farm, and not taken there by the robbers. The third item was the Monopoly set.

1964 - 14 April

Summing up by Justice Edmund Davies. End of Biggs' second trial.

1964 - 15 April

Guilty verdict for Biggs after just 92 minutes of jury deliberation. The Judge spends the rest of the day hearing the past history of the convicted men and speeches by defence counsel in mitigation.

1964 - Thursday, 16 April

The court reconvenes at 10.30 am. The gang is not taken back to the court where the trial was held, but instead are taken instead to the Assizes where they can all be held and locked in the cells before being brought in to court one by one for sentencing.

Mr Justice Edmund Davies passes sentence on the Great Train Robbery Gang. It takes him just 28 minutes to sentence 12 of the men. Most of the sentences are for two concurrent sentences, the crimes being: 'robbery – being armed with an offensive weapon' (30 years / 10,957 days) and 'conspire / robbery with violence' (25 years / 9,130 days).

Seven of gang get 30-year sentences, two get 25 years, one gets 24 years, one gets 20 years and one gets three years. The order of sentencing is Roger Cordrey (20 years) / William Boal (24 years) / Charlie Wilson (30 years) / Ronald Biggs (30 years) / Thomas Wisbey (30 years) / Robert Welch (30 years) / James Hussey (30 years) / Roy James (30 years) / Gordon Goody (30 years) / Brian Field (25 years) / Leonard Field (25 years) / John Wheater (3 years).

Twelve men are jailed for a total of 307 years, although the total sentences are for 573 years as some sentences run concurrently. On appeal they will be reduced from 307 years to 251 years.

Alfred and Mary Pilgrim, who are related to Cordrey, are cleared of receiving money from the robbery. Alfred Pilgrim collapses on leaving the court.

The Great Train Robbery trial has lasted for 51 workings days over a period of 10 weeks. Evidence had been heard from 264 witnesses, and an estimated 2.5 million words had been spoken. There were 2,350 witness statements and 1,700 exhibits. The words filled over 30,000 foolscap pages. The cost of the trial was estimated at £38,733 (about £650,000 by 2013 values). The 12 jurors, all men, were paid 50 shillings a day (about £40 in 2013 values).

At no point in the trial was any evidence presented to prove that any of the accused had been at the scene of the robbery on the morning of 8 August 1963.

The trial over, the gang is split up amongst some of Britain's most secure prisons. Reynolds watches the news of the sentencing on the 6 pm BBC TV News. His comment is: "They have created a monster that will haunt them forever."

The Rolling Stones release their debut album.

1964 - 17 April
Much of the media is questioning the sentences. The Daily Mirror's leader is fairly typical:

Crime and Punishment

The whole country is arguing today about the tremendously long sentences imposed on the Great Train Robbery criminals. People everywhere are puzzled by one glaring contrast. It is this: An evildoer convicted of conspiracy and robbery as in the Train Case can-lie sentenced to thirty years, which, with normal remission, means serving twenty years in prison. But an evildoer convicted of murder if jailed for life is unlikely to serve more than fifteen years.

Does this mean that stealing banknotes is regarded as being more wicked than murdering somebody?

What is the real purpose of the punishment in both cases? To mete out retribution? To deter others? To reform the criminal? Are the present methods of dealing with criminals effective in any case?

Fundamental and far-reaching, questions like these will be examined by the Royal Commission on crime and punishment announced by the Prime Minister yesterday. Everybody will welcome this important move.

The Guardian stated: "...the sentences are out of proportion with everything except the value of the property involved."

Back on 30 September 1963, Mr Justice Edmund Davies, had declared that a sentence of 15 years was "excessive" for a man involved in a robbery where a person was shot and killed, and had reduced it to 10 years. The robbers had expected to find £6,000 on the premises but only stole £517.

In 1968, when Reynolds is captured, it is noted in the press that a night porter who set fire to a Brighton Hotel to get rid of some late customers, and who caused the death of seven people, is sentenced to just five years. A man, who kills a barmaid by putting cyanide in her Guinness because she did not serve him a sandwich, also gets five years.

DAILY SKETCH

Friday, April 17, 1964   Price Threepence ★★★   WEATHER: Sunny and warm

30 YEARS

ALL BRITAIN ARGUES IS THIS TOO HARSH?

For	Against	For	Against	For	Against
Mrs. Kay Searle, housewife: "You expect to have to pay for it."	Mr. Geoff Harris, 30, dancer: "I'm surprised. Very heavy."	Miss Pat Swann, 25, secretary, "I think deserved?"	Miss Vicky Searle, 19, secretary: "I think they're far too much."	John Starling, 18: "Biggest raid, biggest sentence. That's fair."	Mrs. Elizabeth Lacey, 54, housewife: "The sentences are awful."
Mr. Brian Cawkwell, 26, civil servant: "I think it's excellent."	Miss Margaret Grad, 19, Clerk: "They're far too heavy..."	Mr. Laurence Packer, 52, stationer: Orpington: "Good idea."	Mr. Colin Stevenson, 20, fireman: "Ten years was enough."	Mrs. Hilda Pitts 60, housewife: "Not enough."	Mr. John Rattray, 36, potato market porter: "It's certainly too much."
Mrs. Pearl Mather, 33, confectioner: "It's what they deserved."	Christopher Brewer, aged 17, a solicitor's clerk: "Too stiff."	Miss Barbara Sheppard 40: "Get tough with them."	Mr. Douglas Lawrence, 40, sales supervisor: "Too heavy."	Mr. Peter Venner, 21, Clerk: "I agree with the sentences.	Miss Carol Sandeman, 21, studio manager: "It's a lifetime."
Mr. Tony Cranpin, 26, manufacturing optician: "The risk they take."	Mrs. Eileen Goddard, housewife: "I think they're very severe."	Ian Williams, 17, railway fireman: "I'd have given a bit more."	Mr. Brian Bussell, 47, accountant: "Fantastic. They're not deserved."	Mr. C. Burdett, 20, ex-Undergrad: "They won't serve full time."	Mr. Chris Ethell, 22, laboratory technician: "It's a bit high."

SKETCH REPORTERS

THIRTY years. Too severe? Or fair enough? The argument raged all over Britain last night after 30-year sentences were passed on seven men in the Great Train Robbery.

Some people thought the robbers asked for what they got. Others compared the 30-year sentences to those passed in murder cases and cases of sexual offences against children.

While the argument went on detectives waited for a call from a prison cell.

They believe that under the impact of the punishment one or more of the seven may break down—and give vital leads to the missing £2,300,000.

Or that a wife in the know will come forward to flush out the money and more members of the gang still on the run.

A clear indication was given by Mr. Justice Edmund Davies in court at Aylesbury, Bucks, when he spoke first of all to 42-year-old florist Roger John Cordrey—who received 20 years.

The judge said: "You are one of the exceptions."

Cordrey, he said, had helped the police and told them where to find £80,000 of the £2,631,000 money from the train.

The end of the trial did not mean the end of the probe.

There is still the mystery of:—

THE UNIFORMS. Detectives are seeking an Army quartermaster who supplied the gang with a set of soldiers' uniforms as part of the get-away plan.

The gang wore them under overalls when they drove 25 miles from the robbery scene to their hideout at Leatherslade Farm.

The 11 greedy men and one solicitor
PAGE 11

What the drip, drip, drip of years can do
PAGE 12

CONVOY

They had bought an ex-Army three-ton truck and two Landrovers.

After loading up 120 mailbags they stripped off their overalls and formed up in convoy.

An "officer" sat beside each driver in private's uniform.

A "sergeant" sat in the back of the truck with his "platoon of soldiers." The convoy was led by a "corporal despatch rider." They knew that no one

Back Page

FOUL PLAY

Not just the robbers
not playing by the rules

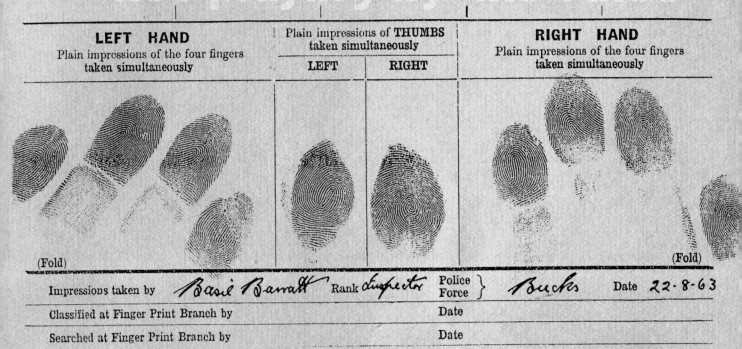

LEFT HAND Plain impressions of the four fingers taken simultaneously	Plain impressions of THUMBS taken simultaneously		RIGHT HAND Plain impressions of the four fingers taken simultaneously
	LEFT	RIGHT	

(Fold) (Fold)

Impressions taken by *Basil Barratt* Rank *Inspector* Police Force } *Bucks* Date 22·8·63

Classified at Finger Print Branch by _____ Date _____

Searched at Finger Print Branch by _____ Date _____

Many have speculated about the authenticity of some of the evidence presented at the trial, especially that against William Boal and Gordon Goody.

Boal was in the company of Roger Cordrey, one of the train robbers, when he was arrested. Boal had paid three months in advance for the rental of a garage, but unluckily the owner, being a policeman's widow, felt something was wrong and contacted the police. Between two vehicles, the police found a total of £141,000, and Boal was arrested along with Cordrey and convicted for conspiracy to rob, receiving a twenty-four year sentence for his trouble. On appeal, this was reduced to fourteen when the appeal court felt something was wrong when even the prosecution admitted that it was 'unhappy' with Boal's case and the scientific evidence used in the

trial. It was not mentioned that the same evidence was used to convict Goody.

Boal was never at the scene of the robbery, or the farm, and had no involvement in the planning, or met any of the other robbers other than Cordrey. He had only agreed to meet Cordrey on the day after the Great Train Robbery to get him to repay £650 that he owed him. But Boal got far more than he bargained for and was to die in prison an innocent man.

By pleading not guilty, the robbers were unable at the time to verify Boal's non-involvement. Cordrey,

Innocent Bill Boal

having pleaded guilty to conspiracy to rob, could have verified Boal's innocence, but his solicitors decided that this would put him in the position of being asked who was involved and who wasn't. His failure to comply could have resulted in him losing any advantage he already had in having pleaded guilty.

The evidence against Boal comprised solely of a small watch winder, found in his pocket, with yellow paint within the grooves. The prosecution claimed the paint was the same as that found at the farm. The paint used on the gang's lorry. As Boal had never been at the farm, this was a total mystery.

Det Supt Malcolm Fewtrell always believed in Boal's innocence and that the evidence was suspect. Not only against Boal, also Goody. Fewtrell was sure Goody was involved, but told Nick Reynolds that he felt the evidence had been cooked up by the Flying Squad, sometimes known as the 'dirty tricks brigade'.

In Goody's case, forensic expert, Dr Holden, found yellow and khaki paint on a pair of shoes; stating it was the same paint found on Boal and in the garage at the farm. The same yellow paint was allegedly found on a brake pedal, although there was none

underneath, as you would expect from where the foot had had to rest. It is also a fact that Goody never drove any of the vehicles.

Goody freely admits to being one of the gang and being at Leatherslade Farm, but is resolute that he was fitted up. In court, forensic claims that the paint on his shoes matched that found at the farm, were refuted by independent experts, (spectrum analysis proving a non-match).

Goody's landlord also stated that he saw no paint on the shoes, before the police took them. Despite this, and the fact there was no other evidence on Goody linking him to the farm, he was still convicted of the robbery.

The police forensics expert, Dr Holden, who had found the shoes, had been humiliated by Goody during the London airport robbery trial. By bribing a policeman, Goody had managed to substitute his bowler hat, (left in the BOAC lobby) for one that was too big for him. When asked to put it on, the court erupted in laughter as the hat fell over his ears, proving he was not the owner.

Goody was acquitted but on leaving the court picked up the chain that had been used to secure the gate that the robbers had used to exit the airport. Triumphantly he declared 'so much for your experts', as he proceeded to show that a hidden link had divided the chain. Goody has always regretted this act of showmanship, and cites it as the reason the police did anything they could in order to make sure he didn't make a fool out of them again.

To the public, Det Supts Butler and Williams had appeared successful in arresting the robbers, but to their discredit, very little of the money had been recovered. Then, on 10 December 1963, money was found in a Great Dover Street phone box. The money had been deposited there by Freddie Foreman, acting as a go between for one of the robbers still to be arrested, but a focus of police inquiries. This was part of a secret deal arranged with Williams who had a reputation for having many underworld contacts who trusted him.

Butler and Williams were sure the suspect was part of the gang, as he was on two informants' lists, but had insufficient evidence to charge him. Incredibly it was agreed that if the suspect gave back part of the money, enquiries would cease. And they did.

When the amount found was announced, Det Supt Fewtrell in Buckinghamshire smelt a rat' as there was no way that the money could have been counted so quickly. Somebody in authority had to know the amount in advance. His suspicions were confirmed when he received the damp bundles, with some of the notes still stuck together. It took two full days with experienced bank tellers to confirm the total was £47,245.

When James White was arrested just over two years later, he received a fifteen year sentence, half that of his comrades. Buster Edwards, now disillusioned with life on the run in Mexico, called Foreman to arrange another deal with Williams. The deal was for Edwards to give himself up, and for Williams to tell the court that Edwards had only had a minor role in the robbery. Edwards

still got twelve years, which is considerably more than he had hoped for, but it was still a lot better than the thirty the others got.

If the robbers' case were to be tried today, it's doubtful that as many would have been sentenced. The police had not really done any sleuthing-informers had simply provided a list of who to look for. However, there was no fingerprint or other evidence at the actual scene of the robbery.

At the trial all the fingerprint evidence presented was found at Leatherslade Farm, and (other than Wisbey and Wilson), all the prints had been found on moveable objects. Objects that could have been brought to the farm at any time with the prints already on them.

This was John Daly's defence after his prints were being found on a Monopoly card, but nowhere else. He was acquitted. This should have established that prints on immoveable objects did not prove where someone might have been.

Even if they had all left prints at the farm on immoveable objects, it still should not have been taken as proof beyond reasonable doubt that they had robbed the train. Others, including Ronnie Biggs, should have got the same result as Daly, or at the very least not have been charged with the robbery.

Fewtrell never could believe that a gang that had done such an expert job on the train would have been so careless as to leave so many prints at the farm. Neither could the robbers who claimed that, after having wiped the place down several times, the prints must have been placed there.

Nonetheless, following Butler's orders, 'don't come out until you have found something', the forensics team did find the prints. 311 fingerprints in total, and another 56 palm prints.

Nick Reynolds once asked Fewtrell if it was possible that some of the prints may have been put there, as they can be transferred with sticky tape, especially from and onto a glasslike surface? Were some prints placed on the moveable objects back at the Yard?

Fewtrell baulked at the notion, despite his suspicions that foul play had taken place with Boal and Goody, and that Maurice Ray, head of the fingerprint department, and an avid print collector, was a regular at the Marlborough in Chelsea, frequented by many aspiring villains including Bruce Reynolds and a number of the robbers.

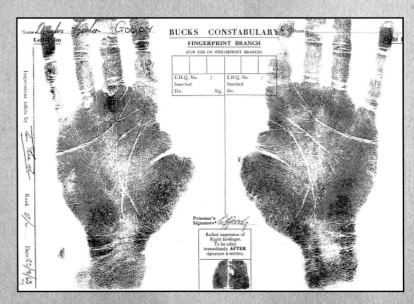

Driver Jack Mills and family

The premises would have proved very suitable for adding to his collection - as glasses make excellent subjects for a full set of prints!

'The suspect paint issue is crucial,' explained Bruce Reynolds. 'If this was part of a fabrication of incriminating evidence to seek a successful prosecution, the corollary must be drawn that the fingerprints may be suspect too.'

This does raise the question that if the prints were planted, then why, with the exception of the suspect who paid £ 50,000, were the other chief suspects not fitted up? And why did the police never bother to charge the back up train driver that Biggs had brought along and who was easy enough to find? The jury is out on both questions.

Another contentious aspect of the train robbery is the driver, Jack Mills. There is no doubt that he was struck, but there is a lot more to it that has been largely ignored.

After Mills died in 1970, Peta Fordham, a barrister's wife at the trial and the author of 'A Robbers Tale, wrote a letter to the Times, stating that now Mills was deceased she could make public a secret he had made her keep.

She had asked Mills if it was true what the robbers had said, that the worst of his injuries resulted from a fall, and not from the blow on the head. After making her promise she wouldn't print what he said until he was dead, he told her: 'They hit my scalp and it bled a lot, but when I stumbled and I caught the back of my head here. [and he indicated the curved steel dashboard]. They say this was the bad injury'.

Fordham asked Mills why he did not mention this in court, or repeat his first statement made to one journalist that the robbers treated him 'like a gentlemen.' This would have suggested to the court that the robbers had not meant the violence, and although it would not have made

a difference to their guilt, it might have made a difference to the sentencing. Mills, Fordham said, became very agitated and begged her not to ever repeat what he had said as: 'I have been warned that my pension will be affected if this comes out.'

Reynolds view was that it was 'tragic' how they used Mills. Reynolds added: 'Instead of a bravery award, he was pressured to suppress evidence, and had to live with the fact this was pivotal in justifying the draconian sentences. He must have been in fear of retribution, for the rest of his life. He was broken by his own side - not us.'

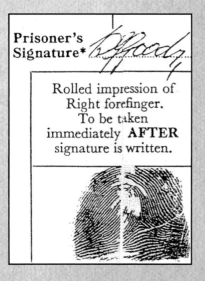

Prisoner's Signature*

Rolled impression of Right forefinger. To be taken immediately **AFTER** signature is written.

Mills spent the rest of his life following the robbery doing light duties, shunting trains on full wages, and when he died seven years after the robbery, the coroner stated that he was aware of Mills involvement in the robbery and he was satisfied this it had nothing to do with his death, which was caused by chronic lymphatic pneumonia. A fact often ignored by sections of the press when it does not fit their agenda or stance on the robbery.

Bruce Reynolds
Thoughts & Deeds

Balzac noted that: 'behind every great fortune there is a great crime' and it always stuck me that I belonged to the greatest nation of thieves in history. From Sir Francis Drake, plundering the Spanish Main and the Americas, the real basis of our empire has always been the acquisition of loot.

As a professional thief I always looked for the big coup, the one spectacular job that I might retire on. I remember a cellmate who implored: 'you've got to sack a city, Bruce.' So, rather foolishly, perhaps, I saw myself as an adventurer, as part of a tradition.

Standing by Bridego Bridge that night, waiting for the Glasgow to Euston mail train, I imagined myself as Lawrence of Arabia on the Hejaz Railway, on a guerrilla operation behind enemy lines. Of course this 'enemy' was our own Establishment. We struck at the heart of it - this was government money. It was this, and the very grandiosity of our scheme, that really got us into trouble.

The media has called me many things over the years, the mastermind, the brains, the leader of the gang, but these are all crass and stereotypical titles. If I had to describe my position on the train I would say I was the dynamo, the chief architect.

For me the planning was a terrific buzz, getting into the minutia. And the train robbery allowed me to indulge in other fantasies. Being an SAS Major was one of those; having had a deep admiration for Stirling the 'Phantom Major', and the long-range desert group - his embryonic Special Forces.

Robbery mythology has it that I used to claim that I was a major in the British Army, but it was my partner-in-crime, Terry Hogan, who started that rumour. One night in the Star Tavern, when wearing an army officer's camel coat, and being tall and cutting a rakish figure, I attracted the attention of

someone who asked Terry: 'who is that man?' Terry replied, 'oh, him, he's the youngest major in the British army'.

Naturally when the robbery took place I knew who I was going to be, but couldn't have dreamt that my affectation would prompt headlines like: 'Hunt for Commando Major'. Although I was thrilled at the time, I did not know that, unlike normal robberies, this one wouldn't die down in a few weeks and that it would inevitably become the world's first mass media crime. I was taken aback when the papers published our faces as being 'wanted' - this was unprecedented, as it could have potentially biased any future jurors. I suppose this was a totally new game, with new rules.

Another surprise, (other than the sentences), was hearing that Interpol had gathered six names of the most wanted men in the world. For the first time in history they were planning to beam their images across the globe via the recently launched Telstar satellite. To my horror I was one of the six, but to my joy the transmission in Mexico, where I was then hiding, was on an early Sunday morning, when none of my new friends would be awake.

In Rio, as we swapped on-the-run yarns, I remember saying to Ronnie, (the first time I had seen him in 29 years) that the press was Frankenstein and we became its monster. Neither of us could have imagined when we were together in Borstal that one day we would create such a brouhaha. It was surreal.

Bruce and Frances Reynolds in1960

Media hype of the train robbery was to inspire various movie crime capers, and if my real life on the run pursued by Tommy Butler the 'Old Grey Fox' wasn't enough, my fictitious alter ego, Johnny Rainbow, has been hunted down by Inspector Clouseau and the Men from Uncle, amongst others. Peta Fordham referred to me as the 'Napoleon of Crime,' and I've read reports, that my wanted poster was the inspiration for Michael Caine wearing horn-rimmed glasses as Harry Palmer. Whatever, it is somewhat preferable to another story, that I was Gerry Anderson's inspiration for the stuttering 'Thunderbirds' scientist Brains!

Back in the 60's the Great Train Robbery was hyped as 'The Crime of the Century' and 'worlds greatest heist. Recent efforts seem more focused on debunking the crime and its title, as if the robbers themselves had bestowed the word 'great'.

Maybe it is because the robbery has been retold so many times that publishers look for a new angle. Suggestions that we were bunglers, and that the police were more like Keystone Cops are all part of this new trend. Either way, bunglers or not we stole the money; Keystone Cops or not, they caught us. Quite frankly, the police were quite happy to have the press big us up as it made them look better, and also covered up the fact that the post office was completely unprepared for the robbery.

To say I have no regrets would be facile and contrived. I have regrets though you can't go back. What has been has been. It's ineradicable. Contrary to some reports, I always regretted that train driver Mills was struck, and have expressed so in writing and on national television, accepting responsibility as chief of the operation. It shouldn't have happened, and was completely unnecessary. It undermined my orders, and certainly wasn't part of the plan.

Mills was supposed to drive the train, with our back up driver in reserve should Mills refuse. At the time the assault took place I was not on the train, but up on the embankment. However when I did go up to the train I saw Mills handcuffed to fireman Whitby sitting on the grass verge with a bloodied handkerchief to his head. I asked him if he was okay, to which he said he was. To be honest, other than shaking my head I thought no more about it.

There have been claims that more violence was used during the robbery than earlier reported, and that other postal workers were injured. If that had been the case, the prosecution would undoubtedly have used this evidence – just as they used Jack Mills, to prove that this was not a case of romantic daredevilry, but a heinous crime of extreme violence. Invariably there was no mention of this in court. I leave you to decide for yourselves as to the truth.

One of the most frequent questions I still get asked is: would I do it again despite how things turned out? A hypothetical question and my answer would usually be: 'well if I was thirty again, yes, but not now'. However, I had to think again when I read Andrew Cook's book on the closed investigation files. I finally realised how the odds were stacked against us, and what madness it was to take on something of this scale. The same kind of madness, I guess, it takes one to bivouac 13,000 feet up the north face of the Eiger in winter.

Fifty years on many have feasted on the bones of the Great Train Robbery. One could be forgiven for thinking that there's precious little flesh left to chew on. However just like the Xmas turkey, when you think the carcass has been stripped bare, a renewed investigation can reveal some of the most exquisite morsels, as you will read here.

The identities of the Ulsterman, back-up train driver, Jack Mills' assailant, and the three who got away have all yet to be officially revealed. This is also the case with the 'squealers', who gave the police invaluable inside information. Perhaps these details will finally come to light, but for now I am not the one to give you the answers.

Ten years ago it was the fortieth anniversary of the train robbery. Then I was asked, much to my surprise, to be the guest of honour at a fundraising fete in Oakley, Buckinghamshire. The village lays claim to being the nearest place to our hideout at Leatherslade Farm. The local council had refused to help fund necessary repairs for the village hall roof, and so they asked if I would help raise the money. It was strange to be asked back, rather like 'come back, all is forgiven', but I guess it's part of their history and the people recognise I was part of that history.

It was a great day and I got re-acquainted with an ex-police officer, John Woolley, the constable who first found the farm, and five years later happened to be handcuffed to me as I left Aylesbury Court. We had a good laugh about the old times when hunter and prey shared a mutual, if grudging respect.

This year will be the fiftieth anniversary of the robbery, although my feelings are quite ambivalent. I will not be celebrating it; I've never celebrated it. As for the robbery itself, I'm neither ashamed of it nor proud of it. I've paid the penalty.

Like the 300 Spartans at Thermopylae, we took on enormous odds, managed a victory of sorts and then ultimately fell. People need to invent mythical qualities for their heroes. And their villains. They want them to be larger than life, bigger than they really are. Something that they themselves are not, but aspire to, or are envious of.

Personally, I was always searching for El Gordo - the big one; the criminal Holy Grail; for the mystical that has no name yet exists forever in the hearts and minds of the adventurer. To this end I have been accused of being a fantasist and romantic dreamer, well, mea culpa.

At least I made my mark. I lived out my dreams, even if they didn't end as I had hoped. And if they had, perhaps I would have got restless and risked it all again for another crazy adventure, seeking Eldorado. C'est la vie!

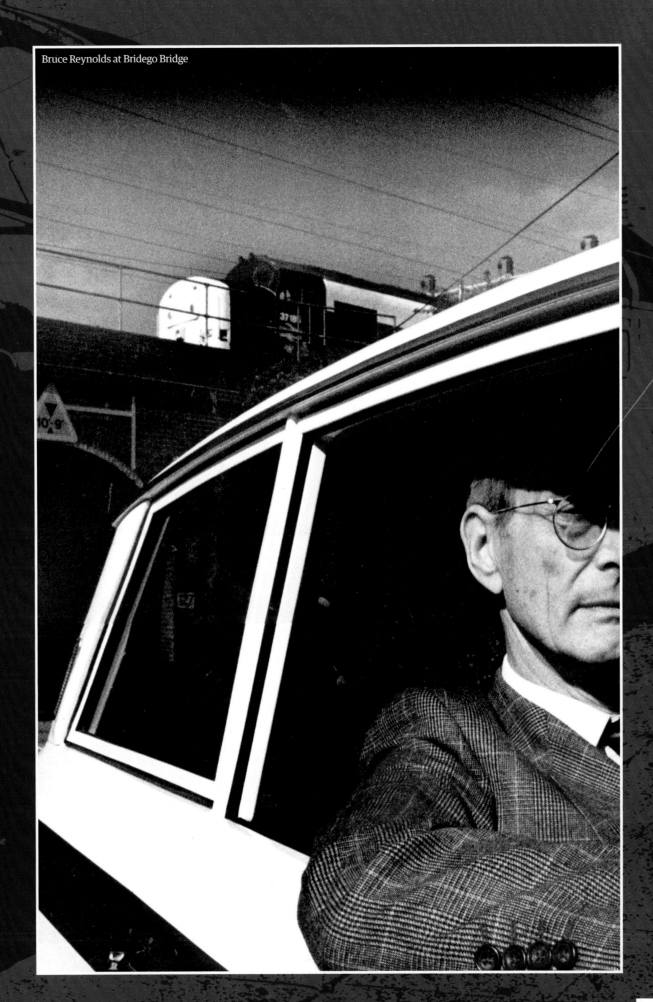

Bruce Reynolds at Bridego Bridge

The Story that refuses to die.....

Soundtrack to the Great Train Robbery

It all started in the 1960's when the cast of the popular BBC TV show *Z Cars* recorded a song about the Great Train Robbery, beginning with the shows signature opening, Calling all Cars.

In 1967 Jim O'Connor penned, *Have You Seen Bruce Richard Reynolds*. The song was no doubt inspired by the many newspapers printing his visage and postulating on his whereabouts. One report has it someone found scrawled on the wall of a hut in the desert the words, 'Bruce Reynolds was here!' On one comic occasion, Det Supt Tommy Butler, was scouring the beaches with binoculars, looking for Reynolds in the south of France. That is, until Gendarmes arrested him, suspecting him of being a Peeping Tom!

The song was recorded by acclaimed folk singer Nigel Denver on his album Rebellion. Denver was a folk purist and strong Scottish republican. The song, inaccurate in parts, gives insight into how the media portrayal of Reynolds was perceived by Denver at the time, whilst recruiting Reynolds into the traditional pantheon of outlaws honoured by folk music.

In 2001 the band Alabama 3, responsible for *The Sopranos*

Have You Seen Bruce Richard Reynolds?

Jim O'Connor

Have you seen Bruce Richard Reynolds he's a man they'd like to find
They say in the great mail robbery he was the master mind
His gang planned the greatest raid the world had ever known
They've stolen 2½ million quid and now the birds have flown

Reynolds was the leader of a South-West London gang
While doing time in prison he heard about a plan
To rob a train but it needed brains, so Reynolds often said
When I leave the 'pen', me and my men will do the job instead

When his time was over Reynolds started on his scheme
He combed the London underworld to find a daring team
He recruited all the experts, a partnership was made
And by August '63 the scene was set for Reynolds' raid

In the early hours of August 8th the raid went like a dream
A hundred and twenty mail bags were stolen by the team
The hounds began their chase but the fox was in his lair
Have you seen Bruce Richard Reynolds, he's now a millionaire?

"They've robbed the mail train" was the cry the papers spread next day
They've stolen 2½ million pounds and all got clean away
But the robbers left their fingerprints, twelve men were soon on charge
But they've only caught the brawn because the brain is still at large

"It's clear to me" the judge he said "an example must be made
It's time to count the cost of the dangerous game you've played
You men are brilliant criminals but the Queen's law must prevail
So I'll rob you now of 30 years so you can rot in jail"

Through the grapevine went the word that Bruce had made a vow
"You've not grassed on me" he said "I'll not desert you now
Iron bars and prison walls, they don't bother me
I've robbed the mail so I'll rob a jail to set my raiders free"

In August '64 Charlie Wilson left his cell
And by July of '65 Biggs had left as well
Have you seen Bruce Richard Reynolds, he's a master mind you know
He's breaking into jails and letting the robbers go

theme tune and with whom Nick Reynolds performs and record, recorded the song for their album *Outlaw*. The concept of the album pays homage to Britain's outlaws turned folk heroes, such as Robin Hood, Dick Turpin and the train robbers. The cover features a baby in a cowboy hat surrounded by money and a toy train set, representing a young Bruce Reynolds.

Reynolds also contributed to the track by providing a narrative roll call of the Wild West's most notorious train robbers. He also appears performing the song in the Alabama 3 film *Outlaw*.

In 1967 the soundtrack for *Robbery* was released. Johnny Keating, who was legendary within big band and jazz circles in both the UK and America during the 1950s, '60s and '70s, wrote the score. Keating's remarkable gifts as a composer-arranger became world-renowned. His score for the 1967 UK crime-thriller film *Robbery* is arguably his best.

In 1971 American rock band Mountain, released *The Great Train Robbery* on their album entitled *Nantucket Sleigh Ride*, the title track of which was used as the theme to popular UK political programme *Weekend World*. The album title refers to the slang term for a boat dragged by a harpooned whale, an interesting metaphor as Reynolds often described the train robbery as Moby Dick and himself as Captain Ahab.

Once again Johnny Rainbow makes an appearance indicating that this intriguing fictional character had by now become embedded into train robbery mythology, even across the Atlantic.

Do you remember The Great Train Robbery?
How it all happened, back in '63
When Johnny Rainbow took his band of brave men
Went down to the crossing to meet that train
When they were sure the time was right

Fourteen men to share seven million
Bound to steal, steal it all and run
Johnny wanted to keep it peaceful
But Wilson cried and though it might have died
You know they had to turn and run

No one knows where the Rainbow is hiding
He's been sure not to tip his hand
He is still living on the fruits of that bloody day
They caught some of his friends, they got some of his money
But they never could catch that man

The affairs of that night will live forever
As the law was breeched in the heart of a thief
Many legends still declare that tragic day
How the iron horse fell, oh I know so well
I was a party to all that grief

The soundtrack to the life of Ronnie Biggs, *Mailbag Blues* was released in 1974. The rock/jazz album features some of Brazil's finest musicians, including American Bassist Bruce Henry.

In 1978 the song *No One is Innocent (A Punk Prayer)* from the Julien Temple film *The Great Rock and Roll Swindle* was released. The song features

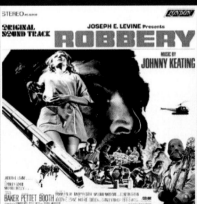
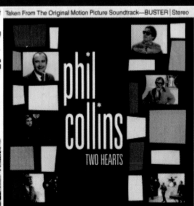

Steve Jones and Paul Cook from the Sex Pistols and Ronnie Biggs, who sings and wrote the lyrics. Distastefully the title was originally to be, **Cosh the Driver**, but Richard Branson at Virgin vetoed this idea.

The record has Sid Vicious on the B-side singing **My Way** and reached number six in the UK charts.

The film itself is a fictionalised account of how Malcolm Maclaren played role of Svengali in creating the pistols, and by conning the record companies and media, made himself rich and turned the group into nihilistic anti-heroes, and the most famous band in the history of Punk Rock.

In 1981 Virgin Records released **Ronnie Biggs was only the Tea-Boy**, which was produced by Tom Newman, famous for Tubular Bells. The song's writers and performers include robber Tommy Wisbey.

In 1985 Paul Hardcastle held the number 1 slot for five weeks in the UK (16 weeks in Holland), with **19**, which sold over 4 million copies worldwide. His follow up single was **Just for Money**. The track strangely combines the Valentine's Day massacre and The Great Train Robbery.

Bob Hoskins and Sir Laurence Olivier appear on the track and the music video, which features clips from the film Robbery and ends with Olivier saying: '...the train robbers were sentenced to a total of 307 years." the frame then cuts to Hoskins behind bars wearing a crown and laughing whilst smoking a large cigar.

Glasgow station;
the Royal Mail train is loaded with
over two and a half million pounds.
That's more money than most people
Can dream of.
But then some people have big dreams.

What if we get caught?
Course we won't!
But say we do?
Don't worry
Just think about the money
Imagine what you can do with it.
This is the last job I'm gonna do.
I'm in for this one

Then I'm out.
It's a life of luxury
My son.
I'm off to Spain and that's it.
Go to Spain
This is gonna be the crime of the century!

In 1986 reggae roots group Black Uhuru, released the album **Brutal** which featured their take on The Great Train Robbery. The album was nominated for a Grammy and the The Great Train Robbery, produced by legendary New York dance producer Arthur Baker, provided them with their second hit single in the UK.

Phil Collins released two singles from the 1988 comic crime film **Buster. Two Hearts** reached number one in both the United States and Canada and won the Golden Globe for Best Original Song

CRIME PAYS

It's a HIT

Sex Pistols

THE GREAT ROCK'N'ROLL SWINDLE

45 RPM
STEREO
A

NO ONE IS INNOCENT
(A Punk Prayer by Ronald Biggs)

Sex Pistols

VS 220

the forthcoming film
THE GREAT ROCK'N'ROLL SWINDLE

and the Grammy for Best Song written for a Motion Picture or Television. The song topped the US Hot 100 for two weeks, the US adult contemporary chart for five weeks, and also reached number six on the UK singles chart. The B-side features Anne Dudley (Art of Noise) and the London Film Orchestra performing *The Robbery*, which is also on the Buster soundtrack.

A Groovy Kind of Love was also hugely successful hitting number one in both the US and UK charts, and it remains the only Collins single to top the charts in both countries. The song earned Collins a Grammy Award nomination for best pop vocal performance in 1989.

Both tracks featured on the soundtrack of *Buster: The Motion Picture*. The opening sequences of the official video show his girlfriend reading a newspaper with the Great Train Robbery in the headlines.

Cult German Punk Band, Die Toten Hosen released *Carnival in Rio (Punk Was)* in 1991, with Ronnie Biggs as writer and lead

vocalist. The B-side included *No One is Innocent* and a version of Eddy Grant's *Police on My Back*. The single was from their album *Learning English Lesson One*.

In 1995 Reynolds had a cameo as a train guard in the music video, *Your Smile* by Brit-pop band Octopus, while Biggs played himself in the video for the Brazilian band Os Intocáveis (The Untouchables) hit protest song, *Ronald Biggs prá presidente (Ronald Biggs for President)*. Biggs would come to meet and know most of the major rock acts that came through Rio de Janeiro. Everyone from the Rolling Stones to, appropriately, The Police.

Biggs' son, Mike, also picked up his father's love of music, and having been spotted on television by the head of CBS Records in Brazil, became part of a children's group called A Turma do Balão Magico (Magic Balloon Gang), with Simony and Toby. The band, which also had its own TV show, sold over 10 million albums between 1984 and 1986, and is the 20th most successful Brazilian acts of all time.

In 1999 the trip hop artist Tricky released his album, *Product of the Environment*. The album featured various underworld figures talking over music including Train Robber Tommy Wisbey.

On 21 July 2009, weeks before Ronnie Biggs 80th birthday, Mick Jones and Gaz Mayall recorded *Ronnie Biggs* at the Rock 'n' Roll Library on 21 July 2009. The record was made as a protest that he should not still be serving time, however just as it was released Justice Secretary Jack Straw announced he would be letting Biggs go. The record also features Dan Donovan, Dudley Sutton and Nick Reynolds.

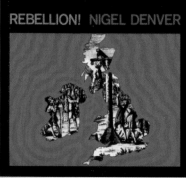

HMP WINSON GREEN
CHARLIE WILSON 12/08/64

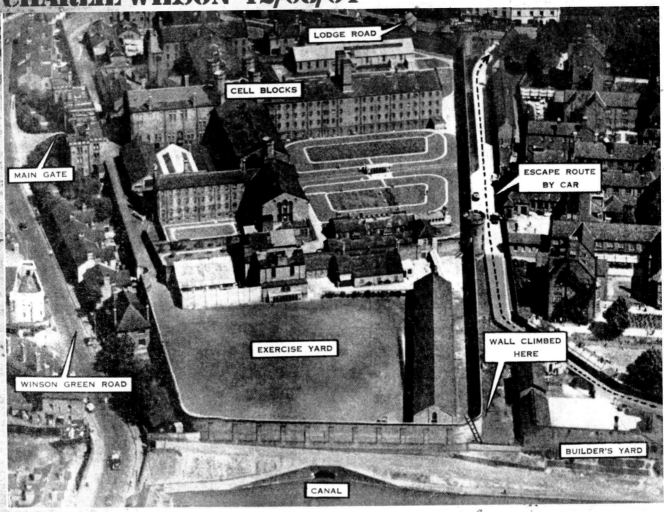

LODGE ROAD

CELL BLOCKS

MAIN GATE

ESCAPE ROUTE BY CAR

EXERCISE YARD

WALL CLIMBED HERE

WINSON GREEN ROAD

BUILDER'S YARD

CANAL

HMP WANDSWORTH
RONNIE BIGGS 08/07/65

MAIN ENTRANCE

HEATHFIELD ROAD

No. 2 EXERCISE YARD

ESCAPE OVER WALL ON TO FURNITURE VAN

TO CLAPHAM JUNCTION

PRISON OFFICERS' QUARTERS

LONDON—PORTSMOUTH RAILWAY LINE

PART FOUR

JUSTICE MUST BE DONE:
Robbers go global - escape, surrender and capture

1964 - 21 April
BBC Two is launched. The launch has been delayed 24 hours due to power cuts.

1964 - 22 April
The Daily Express breaks the story that Scotland Yard has been convinced that another major train robbery was in the planning on the Weymouth – Waterloo line.

1964 - May
Bruce Reynolds prepares to leave the UK. He organises to have his money placed in a Swiss bank account. The fee is 10%.

1964 - 5 May
Butler and Williams go to New Church Road, Camberwell, London SE5 at 6 pm, where they find Henry Smith and Daniel Regan. Smith is taken to Southwark Police Station to be interviewed. His fingerprints and palm prints are taken at Cannon Row police station. No match is found with anything at Leatherslade Farm or linked to the robbery.

1964 - 6 May
Smith, having been held overnight, is taken to Aylesbury and submitted to a number of ID parades. Ten witnesses are called and nobody picks Smith.

Henry Smith

Smith address is re-searched, as is Regans house in Gosport. In Regan's house they find a document that Regan and his associates have bought 32 houses in the Portsmouth and Gosport area, plus a drinking club and a hotel, as well as house in Barking Road where Smith is living. But no physical evidence is found so Butler must let Smith and Regan go.

Biggs is transferred from HMP Lincoln to HMP Chelmsford. Bill Goodwin, who has taken half of Daly's money, dies in Endelstowe, where Daly had hidden the money.

One of the first books about The Great Train Robbery is published. It is written by ex-Scotland Yard Detective Superintendent John Gosling and Dennis Craig. Well researched and informed, for some odd reason it develops the idea that the crime has a super mastermind called Johnny Rainbow. It is almost certain the Johnny Rainbow is Reynolds, but as Reynolds was still on the run there would have been a danger of libelling him. A character called Johnny Rainbow has popped up ever since in *The Man from Uncle* and *Inspector Clouseau*. Even Bart Simpson has been Johnny Rainbow.

1964 - 10 May
Stern magazine publishes the first of two articles about the Great Train Robbery, most of the information for which is supplied by Karin Field.

1964 - 4 June
Bruce Reynolds slips out of the UK. He travels by private plane from Elstree Aerodrome to Gatwick, and on to Ostend and then on by car to Brussels. He pays the pilot £10,000 for the flight out of the UK. About £170,000 at 2013 rates.

1964 - 5 June
Reynolds departs on a Sabena flight from Brussels to Mexico via Montreal where he has to spend the

night when the plane develops a fault. He travels in First Class as "Keith Clement Miller".

1964 - 6 June
Reynolds arrives in Mexico and stays for two weeks at the Hilton while he house hunts. Malcolm Fewtrell publishes *The Train Robbers.*

1964 - 3 July
Frances Reynolds stays back in UK. She goes in to Scotland Yard and asks to see Tommy Butler. "I understand you are looking for me. I'm Frances Reynolds, wife of Bruce Reynolds." Questioned for five hours, Butler threatens to charge her, but can't. She reveals nothing.

Frances can now be reunited with her son, Nick, who has been looked after by Mary Manson for over 10 months. Mary is in Ireland with Nick so Frances flies to Dublin and meets Nick at the Gresham Hotel. Frances takes Nick and Mary to the south of France for two weeks for a holiday. They are followed everywhere. To get to Nice they fly from Shannon to Paris and need to change airports. The French police know of their arrival and escort them across town and to the plane. Frances, Nick and Mary stay in Cannes first at the Martinez and then a flat. They stay for two weeks.

The gang that have been caught and found guilty are reunited at HMP Brixton for their appeal.

1964 - 6 July
The Beatles' film, *A Hard Day's Night* has its premier in London.

1964 - 6-20 July
The appeals are heard for 12 of the convicted men at the Old Bailey in London in front of Justice Widgery, Justice Fenton Atkinson and Justice Lawton. Charlie Wilson refuses to attend the appeal so that he can stay at HMP Winson Green. He knows that the gang are unlikely to be returned to the same prisons after the hearing.

The judges accept the premise of the prosecution that although the robbers were not identified, the fingerprint evidence is sufficient. Brian and Leonard Field have their sentences cut to 5 years after

conspiracy to rob convictions are dropped as no facts have been established that they knew of the intention to stop and rob the train. The prosecution admits that it is "unhappy" with Boal's case and the scientific evidence used in the trial. It is not mentioned that the same evidence was used to convict Goody.

Trying to shift blame, Arthur James QC says Boal should have pleaded guilty to receiving as Cordrey had. Boal's conviction for armed robbery is quashed and in its place there is a 14-year sentence for three charges of receiving. Cordrey also has his sentence reduced to 14 years. A newspaper notes that for some of the men it will be the last time they wear civilian clothes until 1984 at the earliest.

The judges' state: "Last year's £2,500,000 raid was warfare against society and an act of organised banditry touching new depths of lawlessness. In our judgement severe deterrent sentences are necessary to protect the community against these men for a long time." Leave to appeal to the House of Lords is refused.

Biggs is transferred to HMP Wandsworth to serve his sentence. He meets Paul Seabourne. Jimmy Hussey is sent to Walton Jail in Liverpool; Bob Welch is sent to Shrewsbury; Gordon Goody to Strangeways in Manchester; Tommy Wisbey to Oxford; and Roy James to Winchester.

Reynolds follows what is going on from Mexico by listening to the BBC World Service and reading the Telegraph and Times, although the news is days, if not weeks late.

1964 – Late July
Frances Reynolds and her son Nick join Bruce in Mexico. They travel as Angela and Kevin Green. They deliberately do not match Bruce's new name of "Miller" in case they are stopped. Many people will know Frances as Angela for the rest of her life. To make sure they are not followed, Frances and Nick take the ferry from Dover to Ostend, and go by road to Brussels. After two nights in Brussels they take a flight to Mexico, via Montreal. In Mexico City she finds Bruce has set them up in a penthouse apartment at 949 Insurgentes.

1964 - 12 August

Charlie Wilson escapes from HMP Winson Green, Birmingham, just one year and four days after the robbery.

Wilson is sprung from his cell, No 2 on the first floor of C Block, at 3 am He had only been moved to the cell two days earlier. The three men who free Wilson, one of which had been involved in the airport job and the Irish Mail train attempt, use a builders ladder to get into the hospital located next to the prison. A rope ladder is used to scale the wall. They knock out one of two patrolling officers, William Nicholls, for 20 minutes. The raid takes just 15 minutes to complete.

The first call to police about the escape is made from Winson Green at 3.50 am. A special watch is put on all airports and ports. Wilson heads for London, where he stays in a safe house in Knightsbridge for six months.

Winson Green could not explain how a master key was made. It is assumed a guard was bribed to make a copy. The governor, Rundel Harris, and all 120 prison officers, plus civilian staff, are interviewed. Some press speculate that Wilson may have been kidnapped because he knew the location of the

train robbery money. Other gang members receive even tougher treatment in their prisons because of Wilson's escape. Most start to look at ways to escape.

1964 - 13 August

Two men are hanged for murder. The last executions to take place in the British Isles.

1964 - 17 August

Gordon Goody's escape attempt from HMP Strangeways, Manchester, is uncovered.

Eric Flower, a friend of Ronnie Biggs, is sent to HMP Wandsworth. Roy 'Pretty Boy' Shaw also an inmate.

1964 - 18 August

John Maris, the herdsman who "discovered" Leatherslade Farm as the hide out, is given a reward of £10,000 (about £170,000 at 2013 rates) by the Midland Bank. Far more than Mills, Whitby, or anyone else is to receive.

Police believe there will be an attempt to free James Hussey from Liverpool's Walton Jail.

1964 - 22 August

Match of the Day is broadcast on the BBC for the first time.

1964 - 15 September

The Sun replaces the Daily Herald.

1964 - 15 October

Labour defeats the Conservatives at the General Election. Harold Wilson becomes the first Labour Prime Minister in 13 years. He has a majority of five seats.

1964 - 22 October

Now settled in Mexico, Reynolds gets an invitation to a reception to meet Prince Phillip at the British Embassy. He declines the invitation. Reynolds will also meet Michael Caine twice while living in Mexico.

1964 - 9 November

The House of Commons votes to abolish the death penalty for murder.

1965 - January

Tony Benn, who has taken over from Bevin as the Postmaster General, presents Jack Mills with £250 as a reward for his part in the Great Train Robbery. A month later the clearing banks add a further £250 reward.

1965 – 6 February

John Maris, the herdsman who discovered Leatherslade Farm, is cleared of perjury after being taken to court by Geroge Wisbey, brother of train robber Tommy Wisbey.

Maris statement at what he saw at the farm contradicted Wisbey's alibi.

1965 - 9 February

Butler visits Brian Field's father, Reginald, who makes a full statement that it was him who put the bags in Dorking Woods.

1965 – February

Bruce and Frances Reynolds visit Miami and stay at the Fontainebleau Hotel before flying on to Los Angeles to stay at the Ambassador Hotel. In LA Bruce buys a car for Frances. They drive it back to Mexico via Tombstone, Arizona. Terry Hogan contacts Reynolds to see if Edwards and family can join them in Mexico.

1965 – March

Charlie Wilson, who has been living in a safe house in Knightsbridge leaves the UK for the south of France disguised as a teacher on a backpacking holiday. He travels in the name of Ronald Alloway.

1965 April

Paul Seabourne, now a good friend of Ronnie Biggs, is released from HMP Wandsworth. He immediately starts to work of his escape plans for Biggs.

1965 – 2 May

Scotland Yard use the Early Bird satellite to tell TV viewers in America, Canada, Mexico and Europe about Reynolds, Wilson, Edwards, and White, who they are looking for.

1965 - 10 May

Police say they have discovered another plot to free Jimmy Hussey from Walton Jail in Liverpool. The plot involved stealing a master lock from the prison. Peta Fordham publishes *The Robbers Tale*.

1965 – 31 May

Newspapers report that rumours from the underworld suggest that the gang who freed him from prison has murdered Charlie Wilson.

1965 - 9 June

Butler is convinced that Charlie Wilson's children are living with his sister and husband at 29 Laurel Close in Hainault, Essex, and attending a school in Ilford. After being under surveillance for a month the conclusion is that only the wife, husband and son live at the address. Butler believes that Wilson is in London. He also believes that Reynolds is living in the south of France.

1965 - 7 July

The original E(scape) Day for Ronnie Biggs is delayed due to rain. Biggs and Seabourne have planned the escape with the help of Eric Flower, who is serving 12 years for conspiracy to rob. Biggs has also invited Roy Shaw to join the escape, but he declines due to lack of funds.

1965 - 8 July

For an alibi Charmian Biggs takes her children to Whipsnade Zoo. Biggs arrives in the prison workshop in HMP Wandsworth at 2.20 pm having missed the first exercise period. At 2.30 pm Biggs and Flower are moved from the workshop to the exercise yard. Biggs escapes over the 25ft wall at 3.05 pm with the help of a rope ladder. Biggs has personally counted the bricks to work out the height.

A red lorry, parked against the prison wall, and a blue Ford Zephyr are used. The escape is described as: "One of the most daring jail-escape plots of the century."

Eric Flower escapes with Biggs from E Yard along with Robert Anderson and Patrick Doyle who follow them over the wall. Seabourne is helped by Ronnie Leslie, as the getaway driver, and Ronnie Black. The Ford Zephyr is abandoned at Wandsworth Common where they change to a second getaway car.

Leslie and Black are dropped at Tooting tube station. Anderson and Doyle are given the second getaway car, but told to dump it that day. Biggs and Flower are taken to Seabourne's house in Camberwell Grove in Camberwell. Later that day they are transferred by Freddie Foreman and Alfie Gerrard to a safe house in Bermondsey.

1965 - 9 July

Winterfold House in Cranleigh Surrey, the home of Prince Carol of Rumania, is raided by 150 police officers looking for Biggs. The police seal off four square miles of woods, grassland and lanes around the thirty-roomed mansion. Twenty radio cars keep the police squads in touch. The following day the police raid the Upton House Estate, which Prince Carol rents from Poole Council. Police say they were following more tips that Biggs had been seen.

1965 – 14 July

50 airport police swoop at 2am on a DC7 cargo plane at London airport. They believe Biggs is hidden in one of the crates. After an hour the search is called off.

1965 - 15 July

Tommy Wisbey goes on hunger strike for three weeks after being put in solitary confinement for 23 hours a day after Biggs' escape.

1965 - 29 July

The Beatles' film *Help* premieres in London. In one scene the Beatles visit Scotland Yard and John Lennon enquires: "Great Train Robbery – how's that going?"

1965 - 16 August

Paul Seabourne is arrested and later sentenced to four and a half years for helping Biggs to escape. Ronnie Leslie gets three years for helping Seabourne.

Prime Minister Harold Wilson suggests to the Treasury that they secretly replace all banknotes in the hope of flushing out the train robbers and the money from the robbery. The Bank of England dismisses the scheme as impractical. The Prime Minister raises the idea on a number of other occasions.

1965 – July-October

Biggs and Flower are hidden in Bermondsey, Camberwell, Putney, Richmond and Bognor Regis. Hideaways and travel is organised by Freddie Foreman.

1965 September

Butler visits the house in Boscastle where Miss Sleep admits she knew Daly and Black had buried £100,000 in the garden. She also knew Black had stolen £50,000 of it and Goodwin had bricked £50,000 in the wall in the kitchen. Butler now believes that Biggs and Flower are in South Africa.

1965 - August

Charmian gets to visit Biggs in Bognor Regis. It is their first meeting since the escape and their first time together alone since September 1963.

1965 - September - October

Buster Edwards and family fly from Dusseldorf to Mexico City to visit Reynolds.

Biggs and Flower are moved back to London, to the

Biggs and Charmian in Bognor Regis

flat in Camberwell. In early October Biggs is taken to Tilbury Docks with Flower and put on a boat to Antwerp by Foreman. Biggs leaves the UK. He travels as a sports master "Ronald King". They are met in Antwerp by friends of Foreman and driven to Paris.

Butler receives information about a couple living in a caravan camp in Antibes. He believes it to be Reynolds. It is not.

1965 - October - December
Biggs and Flower are based in Rue Vivienne in Paris. They, like Buster Edwards before them, undergo plastic surgery.

Charlie Wilson is now based in Hudson Heights close to Montreal. He visits Bruce Reynolds and Buster Edwards in Mexico. Together they visit Acapulco and stay at Las Brisas.

A waxwork of Biggs and Wilson is put on display in the entrance to Madame Tussauds in London. It is popular to have your photo taken with them.

1965 - 22 December
Eric Flower travels from Paris to Sydney as "Robert Burley" to pave the way for Biggs. Charmian and the children visit Biggs in Paris for Christmas. The family spend Christmas at the Hotel Cécilia at 11 Avenue mac Mahon in the centre of Paris.

1965 - 29 December
Biggs flies from Paris to Sydney via Zurich as "Terence Furminger", a writer born on 13 June 1928.

1965 - 31 December
"Terence Furminger" (Biggs) arrives in Sydney. Biggs and Flower set up home in Botany Bay.

1966 - 31 January
Home Secretary Roy Jenkins allows the press to meet and interview Goody, James and Wisbey in Durham Prison.

1966 - 4 February
Goody, Wisbey and James are transferred at night from Durham to the new purpose built maximum-security block at HMP Parkhurst on the Isle of White. Hussey and Cordrey are transferred from Leicester.

Bruce Reynolds and family visit Charlie Wilson in Canada.

1966 - 8 February
Die Gentlemen bitten zur Kasse (The Gentlemen Require Payment), a three-part mini-series based on the Great Train Robbery, is first broadcast in West Germany on TV Ard. It has a 90% audience share, the highest in German TV history. Horst Tappert plays the part of Michael Donegan, a character that is based on Bruce Reynolds.

For legal reason the producers feel the need to change names. Reynolds and Horst will become good friends. The railway scenes were filmed with a German locomotive close to the town of Moringen near Northeim in southern Lower Saxony.

1966 - 11 February
John Wheater is released from Ford Open Prison. The first release of one of the key names from the robbery.

1966 - March
After their mail is intercepted, Biggs and Flower move from Sydney to Adelaide. "Terence Forminger" becomes "Terence King".

1966 - 20 March
Theft of the World Cup trophy in London.

1966 - 31 March

Labour party wins the General Election. Harold Wilson has an increased majority of 96 seats.

1966 - 4 April

The Great St Trinian's Train Robbery has its premiere in London. The infamous all-girls school foils an attempt by train robbers to recover two and a half million pounds hidden in their school. The cast includes Frankie Howard, Dora Bryan, George Cole, Reg Varney and Terry Scott.

1966 - 8 April

Life magazine runs a major feature "Greatest Train Robbery Legend." It notes: "Two and a Half Years After the Theft of Two Tons of Money, Britons Still Marvel."

1966 - 10 April

Sunday Express publishes photos of the still "wanted" men from the Great Train Robbery.

1966 - 15 April

Time uses the phrase "Swinging London".

1966 - 21 April

Jimmy White is arrested at Claverly Mansions on Grand Parade in Littlestone-on-Sea, Kent. He is living as Bob and Claire Lane. Alfred and Jean Place and Henry Joanna Isaacs are later charged with harbouring Jimmy White.

1966 - 24 April

Bruce Reynolds takes Frances to Las Vegas from Mexico as a birthday treat.

1966 - 24 May

Butler believes Reynolds has returned to the UK after living in the south of France. Charlie Wilson considers moving his family to Mexico.

1966 - 10 June

Charmian, Nick and Chris Biggs leave the UK for Australia. They take a ferry to Ostend and then a car to Brussels. They then fly to Zurich to connect to the BOAC Darwin flight.

1966 - 14 June

The Biggs family is reunited in Australia. Charmian travels as "Mrs Margaret Furminger". Biggs misses them at Darwin Airport and when he finds the hotel Charmian has chosen he discovers (later) that it is holding a convention of Australian police officers.

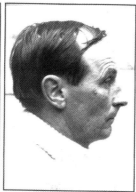

Jimmy White

1966 - 15 June

Tommy Wisbey and two other prison inmates make a four-hour protest on the roof of HMP Leicester over prison conditions and restrictions imposed on them. Wisbey is given nine days in solitary for his part in the protest.

1966 - 20 June

Jimmy White is sentenced to 18 years after pleading guilty to robbery. The prosecution accept his plea of not guilty to conspiracy. In total police recover £45,000 of White's share.

1966 - 30 July

England wins the World Cup beating West Germany.

1966 - 16 September

Buster Edwards and family leave Mexico for the UK. Edwards has decided he wants to give himself up. They first go to Las Vegas, then fly to Brussels, and on to England by car via the Ostend-Dover ferry.

1966 - 19 September

Freddie Foreman has lunch with Tommy Butler and Frank Williams at Simpson's-in-the-Strand to broker a deal for Edwards to give himself up. Edwards surrenders to Williams later that evening at the Prince of Wales pub in Lant Street, SE1. He is arrested. William Green is later charged with harbouring Edwards.

Papers differ in coverage as to if Edwards "surrenders over a cup of tea" or was caught by the Flying Squad who "swooped" in at 3 am.

1966 - 26 September
Lord Edmund Davies, the judge from the Great Train Robbery trial, is named to head the official inquiry into the Aberfan Disaster.

1966 - 22 October
The spy George Blake escapes from HMP Wormwood Scrubs. He is next seen in Moscow.

1966 – 3 November
The Daily Mirror demands on its front-page leader that Britain builds a super prison. What it calls "An island of no escape." It says that Blake, Wilson and Biggs set themselves free "with laughable ease".

1966 - 6 December
Bruce Reynolds and family leave Mexico and drive to visit Charlie Wilson in Canada for Christmas. On 7 December they cross into the US. They then drive to El Paso, Texas, then Dallas and via Oklahoma to Kansas and Illinois and on to Chicago where they spend two days. From Chicago they drive on to Detroit and cross into Canada, and on to Montreal.

1966 - 8-9 December
Ronald 'Buster' Edwards is sentenced to 15 years at Nottingham Assizes. Half of what the other robbers received as a sentence just two years earlier. The judge decides, as had been agreed with Williams, that while Edwards was 'in the hierarchy' he was 'not one of the leading planners.'

1966 - 23 December
Reynolds arrives at Wilson's house in Hudson Heights close to Montreal. Over the holidays Reynolds will seriously consider moving the family to Canada. But he thinks Vancouver may be a better choice. The problem facing Reynolds is that his passport is in the name of "Miller" while Frances and Nick are "Green". The solution will be to return to Europe and get new passports as a married couple with a son.

1967 – January
Reynolds drives his car from Canada to the US and leaves it in a garage in Plattsburg, close to the border. The car is registered to "Keith Miller". The Reynolds then fly to Brussels from Montreal and are surprised when the plane lands at London Airport. They fly on to Brussels and stay at the Westminster Hotel. In Brussels they are given new passports. They are now George and Pauline Firth, while Nick is Colin Firth. They fly back to Canada after Bruce has cut off his beard to morph from Miller to Firth, who was 10 years younger.

1967 - February
Scotland Yard moves from its historic site on Victoria Embankment, the Norman Shaw Buildings, next to Canon Street police station, to a new building at 10 The Broadway, close to St James's Park tube station. During a visit to the new building on 17 May, the Queen is shown items connected to the Great Train Robbery.

1967 - 21 April
Farley Paul Biggs born in Glenelg Community Hospital in Adelaide.

1967 - 23 April

Having decided that Canada does not feel right for them after further problems with the official paper work in Vancouver, Charlie Wilson drives the Reynolds family across the border from Canada to the US where Bruce picks up his car and drives on to New York. It is the end of the Reynolds' Canadian dream.

In New York Reynolds sells his Cadillac and buys a Mustang that he ships to Antwerp. After a few days the family fly to Frankfurt as the Firths, but decide they will need yet another new passport and identity. The new passports have the name of George and Joyce Overton.

1967 - 30 April

Reynolds moves on to the familiar surroundings of the south of France. The family settles in a villa on the road between St Tropez and Ste Maxime. The villa costs £30 per week. Reynolds is down to his last £28,000 from the train robbery (about £420,000 at 2013 values). Reynolds hears Butler is spending his holidays in the south of France looking for him.

1967 - May

After receiving a warning, the Biggs family move from Adelaide to Hibiscus Road in Melbourne. "Terence King" becomes "Terence Cook". Charmian becomes "Sharon".

Brian Field is released. He changes his name by Deed Poll to Brian Mark Carlton. Karin has divorced him and returned to Germany. He marries Sian. Together they work for the Children's Book Centre in Kensington High Street. From 1973 they live at Helston, near the south Cornish coastline.

1967 - June

Wilson flies from Montreal to Nice to visit Reynolds and discuss "business".

1967 - 20 June

Gordon Goody's libel trial gets underway in London. Goody is claiming damages from the publishers of The People for an article printed on 26 July 1964. Wisbey, Welch and Hussey are also suing the publishers. The article had named Goody as taking part in the London airport job and for "coercing an innocent and decent young woman" (Karin Field) in to taking part in the train robbery. He wins the case and is awarded 40 shillings in damages.

1967 - 31 July

Frances Reynolds flies to London with Nick, who needs his tonsils removed. She moves back into the Albert Mews flat, now owned by a friend.

1967 - August

Frances Reynolds and Nick visit Madame Tussauds and see the wax works of Charlie Wilson and Ronnie Biggs. She also notices all the posters for *Robbery* around London.

1967 - 8 August

Robbery, starring Stanley Baker and directed by Peter Yates, opens in London. Producer Michael Deeley had bought the film rights to Peta Fordham's book, *A Robber's Tale*. For legal reasons, the film company decide to make it fictional. An American robber, to be played by Jason Robards, was nearly included in the final script.

1967 - 22 September

Realising he will need to raise more money to live, Reynolds returns to the UK from the south of France. He flies from Brussels to Paris, and on to Shannon. Then by car to Dublin and a flight to London.

Ronnie Biggs in Australia with his sons Nick and Chris

1967 - December

Reynolds moves to a cottage in Newdigate, Dorking, close to Gatwick Airport. The house is owned by Peter Asher, brother of Jane and one half of pop duo Peter & Gordon.

1968 - 2 January

The Reynolds move from Dorking to a flat in Princess Gate Mews, just off Exhibition Road in London. Frances can go out, her disguise is now so good that not even her sister recognises her when they cross in a hotel.

Reynolds uses a system for appointments that he has picked up from a thriller. Each friend and key contact has a copy of the London Underground map where each station is randomly numbered.

To fix a meeting Bruce just has to call and say "nine, one o'clock." He always takes two hours off the time so the meeting would be at station "9" at 11 am. He will be well gone by 1 pm.

1968 - 25 January

Charlie Wilson is arrested in Canada. Detective Chief Superintendant Tommy Butler, supported by the Mounties, makes the arrest. Wilson is arrested at Mountview Ranch in the market town of Rigaud, Quebec. Still using the name of Ronald Allaway, Wilson was with his wife Patricia and three children.

In the house police find an album of photos left behind by Reynolds on his most recent visit. It shows him in Las Vegas, and even in front of his car. The photos are published in the UK press. A Canadian court rules Wilson is an illegal immigrant who can be deported to UK.

By pure chance Biggs meets up in Melbourne with Mike Haynes, one of his best friends from the UK.

1968 - 26 January

From information found in Wilson's house police raid a pub in Kensington and miss Reynolds by ten minutes.

Butler now believes Reynolds is back in the UK and Biggs is in Canada. Reynolds considers a move to Australia not knowing Biggs is already there.

1968 - 27 January

Charlie Wilson is flown back to London on BOAC flight 610 from Montreal. The flight stops at Prestwick where more than twenty reporters and photographers join the flight. Wilson says he wants £30,000 for his story.

1968 - 28 January

While transferring Wilson from London airport to HMP Parkhurst, the Rover car carrying him manages to crash into four other cars when a pedestrian walks onto the A3. Wilson has to be swapped over to a police Humber.

1968 - June

Reynolds decides that he and the family will be safer living outside of London. He spots an ad in The Sunday Times and chooses Villa Cap Martin, a house on a hilltop in Braddons Hill Road East, in Torquay. With its palm tree lined coast Reynolds tells Frances it reminds him of the Riviera. They live as Mr and Mrs Hiller.

Because the house is booked for the summer, the Reynolds family have to move out for six weeks to stay in Teignmouth, with a further six weeks spent at a house in Kew in London.

Daily Mirror

The man Butler of the Yard hunted for 5 years is accused of Great Train Robbery plot

Chief Superintendent Butler of the Yard.

5d. Saturday, November 9, 1968 ✦ No. 20,179

HUGE POLICE GUARD ON BRUCE REYNOLDS

By TOM TULLETT and EDWARD VALE

A MASSIVE security force surrounded the police station where Bruce Reynolds, last of the men sought by police after the Great Train Robbery, was in custody last night.

Several teams of Flying Squad officers, backed up by local police with dogs, surrounded the police station at Aylesbury, Bucks., where Reynolds will stay in the cells until he appears in court today.

Police cars circled the area. And uniformed policemen stood on guard at all the station's entrances and exits.

Reynolds had been taken to Aylesbury after his dramatic dawn arrest at Torquay, Devon, by Detective Chief Superintendent Thomas Butler, the Scotland Yard man who had been seeking him since the £2,500,000 robbery on August 8, 1963.

For more than five years, 37-year-old Reynolds was wanted for questioning in connection with the robbery—the last of fifteen men who figured in police inquiries. Fourteen men were jailed for a total of 284 years.

Ready

Chief Superintendent Butler, 56, head of the Yard's Flying Squad, has led the investigations throughout. He is due to retire next month.

On Thursday evening silver-haired Mr. Butler took his sergeant, Ted

He will appear in court today

said, " Be ready to move in thirty minutes."

Shortly before midnight they drove away from the Yard in a Jaguar, bound for Torquay — 191 miles away—and a meeting with detectives of the Devon and Cornwall constabulary.

Behind them was a team of twelve Flying Squad men in three cars. Each was hand-picked, and each knew Reynolds by sight.

Silence

1968 - 4 August

Bruce Reynolds takes Frances and Nick to visit Bridego Bridge, the scene of the robbery. It is just three days before the 5th anniversary of the robbery.

1968 - 9 September

Reynolds moves back into Villa Cap Martin. He plans to spend the winter in Torquay and then consider a move to Australia in 1969.

1968 - November

Reynolds is stopped by a policeman in Torquay for parking too close to a pedestrian crossing. He has to take his licence in to the local police station.

1968 - 8 November

Bruce Reynolds is arrested at 6.10 am at Villa Cap Martin in Torquay, Devon, by Detective Chief Superintendent Tommy Butler. Reynolds is taken to Aylesbury Police Station and charged at 3.45 pm. Reynolds comment to Butler on his arrest: *"C'est la vie!"*

Butler explains later that he tracked Reynolds down after he had been tipped off that Bruce would be visiting London in November.

The informant even named the pub. They missed Reynolds by just 20 minutes. Butler also knew that

Reynolds had been driving a Mini-Cooper so he got his men to take down the registration number of every Mini parked in that part of Chelsea.

One of them was registered to Angela Hiller from Torquay. The family and description matched Reynolds and so Butler had the phone tapped and the house put under observation until they were certain he was in the house.

1968 - December
Tommy Butler announces during a dinner at the London Hilton to mark the 50th anniversary of the Flying Squad, that he will now retire.

1969 - 14 January
Reynolds, hoping for a sentence similar to Edwards, pleads guilty, also on the understanding that Frances and Nick will not be prosecuted.

He is sentenced to 25 years at Buckinghamshire Assizes by Mr Justice Thompson and sent to HMP Durham.

1969 - 19-26 January
Frances Reynolds' story is published in the UK in the Sunday Mirror and in Germany in Stern. From her fee she buys a flat in Queen's Road, Weybridge. To avoid the press she changes her name to Angela Conway.

A hunt that went around the world . . .

CONTINUED FROM PAGE NINE

FIVE of the many faces of Bruce Reynolds during his five and a half years on the run. Left: Keith Clement Miller the writer. Right: Keith Miller, sales rep.

Five faces of a man on the run

Reynolds after arrest.

AS George Malcolm Firth (left) Reynolds was to spend two years on the Continent. Then he became Terence Overton (right), a businessman.

The Story that refuses to die.....

The Great Train Robbery on Film

The impact of the robbery and media portrayal influenced and inspired a plethora of movies. The classic structure of dogged top policeman chasing a criminal mastermind has always proved to be a successful formula in entertainment.

Arguably without the Great Train Robbery there would have been no *Italian Job*. In the 1965 Bond film *Thunderball*, the robbery is referenced when a member of SPECTRE informs us that they provided the information for the train robbery to a criminal organisation for a fee.

In West Germany in 1966, a three part series entitled *Die Gentlemen Bitten zur Kasse, (The Gentlemen Prefer Cash)* was produced for TV. The series starred Horst Tappert as the character of Bruce Reynolds, a career criminal, with an antiques business as a front. For legal reasons the names were changed. *Die Gentlemen Bitten zur Kasse* was a massive hit and broke viewing records, so it was re-edited into a full-length film and released as *The Great British Train Robbery*.

The German film was in many ways was more realistic than its 1967 British counterpart (*Robbery*), especially as it included the London airport robbery at the beginning, which some of the train robbers had carried out earlier that year. This knowledge had not been confirmed to the British public or police at the time, so it was a bit of a mystery as to how this came to be.

Years later it was revealed the information came from Fields' German wife, Karin. Brian Fields was instrumental in providing the information for both robberies. When Leatherslade was evacuated, he and his wife held a party for some of the robbers

and their wives at his home, which wasn't far from the farm. After Fields' arrest she moved back to Germany and had a relationship with a journalist. He wrote about her story for Stern magazine, and then developed parts of it into the screenplay for *Die Gentlemen Bitten zur Kasse.*

Frances Reynolds also sold her story to Stern, and this too was turned into a screenplay. In 1972,

James Hussey, Bruce Reynolds, Horst Tappert, Buster Edwards, Bridego Bridge

Tappert played Reynolds again for German TV's *Hoopers letzte Jagd (Hooper's Last Hunt)*. Hooper being Butler. This sequel was not as successful as its predecessor.

Horst Tappert, whose career was launched by the mini-series playing a villain, was later to star as Derrick, the Continental Detective, a cult hit that was licensed to 104 countries. In 1998, Reynolds presented Tappert with a lifetime achievement award at a show in Germany. Reynolds was driven onto the stage on the back of a police motorbike, with the trophy in a mailbag.

In 1966, three years after the Great Train Robbery had taken place, *The Great St. Trinian's Train Robbery* was released. A British comedy set in the fictional girl school of St Trinian's; it parodies the technocratic ideas of the Wilson government and its support of the comprehensive school system. One could argue that it also demonstrated that for many the robbery could not have been such a heinous crime if it was to be the subject of a popular comedy in heavily censored times, especially as the robbery was foiled by school girls.

It was the third in the original trilogy of St Trinian films, and the first to be made in colour. It starred George Cole, Frankie Howard, Reg Varney, Dora Bryan and Stratford Johns as the Voice. The film's use of trick gadgets, spoofs the secret gadgets used in the James Bond spy films of the Sixties, while the mastermind conceals his identity, appearing only

as a voice parodying the character of Bond villain Ernst Stavro Blofeld, who was also originally only an unseen voice.

In 1968 actor Stanley Baker co-produced and starred in *Robbery* playing a character based on Bruce Reynolds. In real life, it was known that Baker liked to associate himself with the criminal underworld. In fact previously that year he had starred in a film entitled *The Criminal* and managed an amateur football team Soho Rangers, which included infamous criminals such as Mad Frankie Fraser and gang leader, Eddie Richardson. Baker turned down the role of James Bond, but his production company produced *The Italian Job*.

Robbery is a heavily fictionalised account of the Train Robbery, and starts with a jewel robbery, instead of London Airport, and a high-speed getaway. The film was directed by Peter Yates and notably features a spectacular car chase. The gang escape, but one of the drivers is arrested, echoing events in real life, as driver, Micky Ball, was the only robber caught for the London Airport Robbery.

Robbery was seen by actor Steve McQueen who then got Yates to direct his film, Bullit that features

one of the Silver Screens' greatest car chase scenes. The film ends with the gang getting arrested except for Baker who flies his money out to Switzerland and goes to New York. Interesting to note that in actuality Reynolds had his money transferred to a Swiss bank account and flew out of the country in a private plane to Ostend.

In 1969, David Niven re-enforced the press-inspired notion of a criminal mastermind by playing a criminal genius whose brain was so big that whenever he had a brainwave his head would roll to one side with the weight. The film was a French comedy called *The Brain* and his character was a military officer who had planned The Great Train Robbery in England, and was now planning a similar coup in France. The film also starred French favourite Jean Paul Belmondo.

One early account of the train robbery to appear in a book was **The Great Train Robbery**, written by detectives John Gosling and writer Dennis Craig, and published in 1964. The book claims that the army officer who planned the raid was in fact someone codenamed Johnny Rainbow.

Rainbow then makes another appearance in the 1967 novel **The Rainbow Affair**. The book was a spin-off from the cult American TV series **Man from UNCLE**. Agents Napoleon Solo and Ilya Kuriakin have to track down the man who masterminded the Great Train Robbery before he is affiliated with THRUSH, enemy of UNCLE. Along the way the duo meet up with Britain's most famous fictional sleuths.

This colourful fictional character, inspired by Bruce Reynolds, was to appear again as a criminal mastermind in the 1968 film **Inspector Clouseau**, starring Alan Arkin instead of Peter Sellers in the lead role. In this film Clouseau has to track Rainbow down who is credited with masterminding the Great Train Robbery.

Around the time of the robbery one of the most popular comic shows in England was **Beyond the Fringe** with comedians Peter Cook, Dudley Moore, playwright Alan Bennett and writer Jonathan Miller. One act developed in late 1963 featured a sketch lampooning the police efforts to find the robbers and the mindermast (sic). The revue was widely considered to be ahead of its time, with its unapologetic willingness to debunk figures of authority, something only previously delved into in **The Goon Show** and, arguably, **Hancock's Half Hour**.

This satiric attitude was reinforced in the 1965 Beatles film Help, which has a scene echoing the show when John Lennon (then arguably one of the most famous people on the planet) asks a policeman snidely, 'Great Train Robbery, how's that going then'. One could be forgiven for imagining that Lennon was actually on the robber's side.

In 1975 Larry Lamb starred as Biggs in the BBC film **The Great Paper Chase**. Based on the book **Slip-Up** by Anthony Delano, the film focused on the Fleet Street frenzy when Ronnie Biggs was discovered in Brazil attempting to do a deal with Colin Mackenzie of the Daily Express. He was planning to get money for his family in Australia and then give himself up. Biggs was double crossed, and without contacting Brazilian Authorities, Scotland Yard's Jack Slipper went over to arrest Biggs and bring him back, complete with the media circus in tow. The attempt

Inspector Jacques Clouseau: And now since we are becoming so chummy, perhaps you can tell me about The Great Train Robbery?
Addison Steele: I don't know nothing!
Inspector Jacques Clouseau: He who don't know nothing, must know something, eh?

turned into a farce and Slipper was sent back without his man. The film starred Michael Gambon as Slipper, portraying him as a total buffoon out of his depth.

After the BBC first screened *The Great Paper Chase*, Slipper sued for libel (funded by Jimmy Goldsmith, incidentally), and in 1990 he was awarded £50,000 in damages. The BBC was also ordered to pay costs of more than £400,000. Slipper died in 2005, but the BBC has steadfastly refused to rebroadcast the film.

In 1988 Alan Aykbourne, the celebrated playwright wrote, *Man of the Moment*, considered to be one of his best plays starring Michael Gambon. The play was inspired, by observing the irony of how Buster Edwards, now a flower seller flower, had achieved celeb status and not driver Mills.

This status was generated by the publicity he received as being the subject of the 1988 comedy film *Buster* starring musician Phil Collins, who was a worldwide star at the time and co-starred Julie Walters as his wife. The film also starred Larry Lamb, who had played Biggs in *The Great Paper Chase*, as Reynolds and was based on the life of Edwards and his wife June around the time of the robbery, and their time on the run in Mexico with Reynolds.

June is shown as disliking Mexico and returns home and the film closes with Buster missing her and making a deal with police, before giving himself up. Although most of the film is based on fact, the ending is fictional, as Buster actually left Mexico with June. Both Reynolds and Edwards acted as technical advisors.

The film's profile was raised when news emerged that the movie was intended to have a Royal Premiere with the attendance of Prince Charles and Princess Diana. However the film got more press than it bargained for when critic Alexander Walker dedicated a whole page in the Evening Standard pleading the Royals not to attend.

Under pressure the couple pulled out, but on the night in question, it was evident that there had been no time to change the tickets as the words 'Royal premiere attendance by HRH Charles and HRH Diana', were still visible, despite the attempts to cover them up with a sticker. The film was well received but criticised for its comic tone and likened to a Carry On film.

1988 also saw the release of, *Prisoner of Rio* directed by Lech Majewski, starring Steven Berkoff as a Slipper-type policeman and Paul Freeman as Biggs.

The film was based on a semi-fictional screenplay written by Biggs and Majewski. Set against the stunning backdrop of Rio and the carnival, the plot centres on the relationship Biggs forms with a British detective who has come to extradite him and also recounts his famous kidnapping, albeit in fictional form. It had a limited cinema release and was soon consigned to video. Steven Berkoff found the whole affair incredibly frustrating and wrote an excellent book defining his difficult experiences during the making of the film in his, *I Was a Prisoner of Rio*.

In 2000 the producer of *Buster*, Norma Heyman, produced *Gangster Number One* although the film has nothing to do with the train robbery; Bruce Reynolds was brought on as technical advisor, and personally auditioned and approved Paul Bethany for the title role. Whilst on set Reynolds spent some time with lead actor David Thewlis, who was later to use the experience by putting some of Reynolds' foibles into his character, gang leader Freddie Mays.

In more recent times, ITV produced *Mrs Biggs* based on the life of Charmian Biggs and her time with Ronnie. The series ran

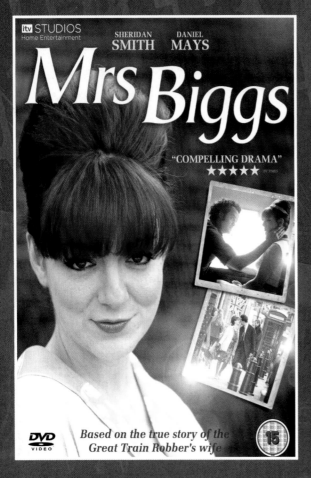

for five episodes in 2012 and starred Sheridan Smith as Charmian and Danny Mays as Ronnie.

Jay Simpson played Bruce Reynolds character and in 2013, Sheridan Smith was awarded a BAFTA for her role. The series claimed it was the "true story", which lead Biggs to comment. "It might be a true story, but it is not mine!"

To mark the 50th anniversary of the robbery, the BBC has commissioned two 90-minute films. **A Robber's** Tale directed by Julian Jarrold tells the story of the gang.

The cast includes Luke Evans (Reynolds), Jack Roth (Wilson), Neil Maskell (Buster), Paul Anderson (Goody), Martin Compston (James), Del Synnott (Brian Field) and Jack Gordon (Biggs).

Film two is **A Copper's Tale**, directed by James Strong, that tells the story of Tommy Butler and his team of detectives. Jim Broadbent plays Butler.

The Great Train Robber has also been the subject matter for more documentaries than most topics. Notable, amongst those screened in the UK, are listed below

The Great Train Robbery	(1964 - World in Action: Season 2, Episode 26)
The Great Train Robbery	(1978 - Man Alive. ITV)
Great Crimes and Trials of the 20th Century	(1993 - Uden Associates)
Underworld	(1994 - BBC)
Once a Thief	(1995 - Everyman / BBC)
I Married a Great Train Robber	(1996 - Channel 4)
My Dad's a Villain	(1999 - Carlton)
World's Most Daring Robberies	(1999 - Channel 4)
The Great Train Robbery Secret History	(1999 - BBC)
I Was a Great Train Robber	(2001 - ITV)
Robberies of the Century	(2001 - Michael Hoff Productions USA)
The Legend of Ronnie Biggs	(2002 - Channel 5)
Days That Shook the World: 8 August 1963	(2004 - History Channel / BBC)
Ronnie Biggs - the Last Escape	(2005 - Sky)
Kidnap Ronnie Biggs	(2005 - Channel 5)
The Great Train Robbery	(2008 - Master Crime Museum)
Buster - Movie Connections	(2009 - BBC)
Ronnie Biggs - Secret Tapes Revealed	(2011 - Channel 5)
The Great Train Robbery's Missing Mastermind	(2012 - Channel 4)
The Great Train Robbery	(2012 - ITV)

The Train Robbery in American Culture

The Great Train Robbery was the title of a 12-minute film produced and directed by Edwin. S. Porter in 1903, which is today regarded as a milestone in movie making. The movie became the first important Western and established the Western as a unique film genre. Its dramatic, narrative structure of 'crime - pursuit - retribution' set the pattern for almost all future Western films.

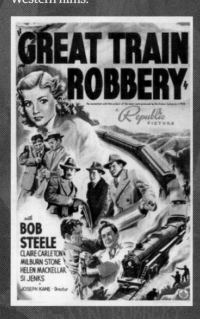

The Great Train Robbery became the American film industry's first great box-office hit earning an estimated $2 million by 1908. Members of the audience often ducked for cover when the main outlaw, appeared to shoot point-blank at them.

In 1926, hoping for the same commercial success, *The Great K & A Train Robbery* was released. The film was a Western based on a true story about a detective preventing a train robbery. The film starred silent movie star Tom Mix.

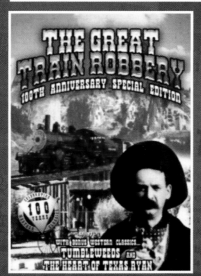

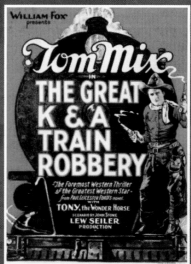

In 1941 Hollywood produced another *The Great Train Robbery*. This was a low budget story about a stolen train full of gold.

In 1955 the title was used for a Halloween episode of the hit TV series *I Love Lucy*, starring Lucille Ball.

And in 1965 we have a cultural crossover as an episode of American cult show *Batman and Robin* was also entitled, *The Great Train Robbery*, the show makes reference to its English counterpart, as the train is carrying money to be destroyed by the banks.

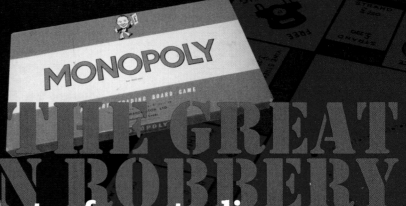

THE GREAT TRAIN ROBBERY

The Story that refuses to die.....

Playing Games with the Great Train Robbery

The game 'Monopoly' always comes to mind when anyone mentions The Great Train Robbery. As legend has it, the robbers played using real money, leaving their fingerprints on parts of the game, leading in some cases to their convictions. Except for those of John Daly, who luckily was the only robber to get acquitted as he managed to convince the jury that his prints were already on the board before it went to the farm. No one there could have imagined that their deeds that night, and that this event would one day in turn be used as the basis for a number of games.

In 1966 following the success of *Die Gentlemen Bitten zur Kasse*, Schmidt Spiele produced a board game in Germany with the same name. The box cover featured a picture from the film, with Horst Tappert as Reynolds, wearing a bowler hat. The aim of the game was to get mailbags to a safe house, and if stopped by police you could bribe your way to continue.

In the early 1970s the British military historian and author Bruce Barrymore Halpenny created *The Great Train Robbery* Board Game, based upon the robbery. The game had a good response in Britain, in a year when the indoor games market had taken a knock.

The famous train artist David Weston was commissioned by the game's inventor to paint the board

In 1999, SCI a leading games company signed up Biggs and Reynolds to produce a Great Train Robbery video game. Previously the company had enjoyed enormous success with the video game *Carmageddon*. However the game never crystallised, but SCI boss Bill Ennis invited Reynolds to join him on the Gumball Rally in 2000.

The Great Brain Robbery, a zombie-themed board game, was inspired by the various great train robberies. The game was designed by James Ernest and released in 2000 by Cheapass Games. It is a Wild West themed sequel to *Give Me the Brain*. Players assume the role of zombies attempting to rob a speeding train full of brains. In 2001 it won the Origins Award for Best Science Fiction or Fantasy Board Game.

game's box. The train, however, was changed from a diesel electric to an old steam engine on Halpenny's orders to add dramatic effect and conjure up images of the Wild West. It was used as a prize on TV shows such as *Tiswas* and *Crackerjack*. It is currently being brought out again by the ANZIO Group after popular demand.

In 2010, The Great Train Robbery was a topic featured in the popular TV quiz show *QI*, hosted by Stephen Fry. The panel was asked what was 'Great' about the train robbers, and then managed to get their facts wrong concerning how Biggs became involved and about the backup driver. Biggs was not in prison, when Reynolds told him about the job, and the driver didn't lie about being able to drive the train.

When the British version of *Trivial Pursuit* came out there were at least two questions regarding the robbery, while Black Uhuru's song *Great Train Robbery* appears on the *Grand Theft Auto; San Andreas* video game soundtrack.

EXHIBIT 'A'

PART FIVE

PAYING A HIGH PRICE:
Freedom for some. Murder, kidnap and death for others

1969 - 4 February
An auction is held in Measham, Burton-on-Trent, Staffs of the personal effects of the Great Train Robbers as well as Reynolds' own household furniture and effects. 128 items are sold for a total of £9,837 (about £130,000 in 2013 values). The Austin-Healey bought by Reynolds for £835 is sold for £930.

1969 - 26 February
The Chief Constable of Durham, Alec Muir, suggests in a speech to the Durham University Liberal Club that the Great Train Robbers should all be shot. "Personally I think society has the right and a duty to eliminate these people who have shown that they are not prepared to play according to the rules." A political storm follows.

After the Chief Constable's speech a poll by newspapers show the train robbers still have the public support. The Evening News, who could not find one person to support Muir's view, notes:

"The general opinion was that the mail gang would be in prison longer than child murderers, and had received sentences out of proportion to sentences for more serious crimes."

1969 5-26 March
Frances Reynolds' story is published in The Australian Women's Weekly over four weeks. It includes photos of Ronnie Biggs. Ironically the paper adds an editorial comment to Frances' story and says: "At the time of writing he (Biggs) is still at large. He is believed to have been narrowly missed by the police in Belgium last month at a place where Reynolds stayed while on the run."

1969 - 7 March
Premier of *The Brain*, a French film starring David Niven and Jean-Paul Belmondo. Niven's character is said to be the brain behind the Great Train Robbery who is planning another robbery in France.

1969 - July
Biggs has a bad car crash in Melbourne that results in a broken jaw and teeth.

1969 - 16 October
A Reuters correspondent drops in at Melbourne Police Headquarters looking for news and sees a memo on a desk that suspects that Biggs is living in Melbourne with his wife and children. The news goes out on the wires and in no time the rest of the media has picked it up. On the evening news Channel Nine shows mug shots of Biggs and Flowers, together with their general description and the information that the police believe Biggs is working as a carpenter in Western Australia.

1969 - 17 October

Early in the morning Charmian drives Biggs to the Alexander Motel in Essenden, close to the airport, where he checks in as Arthur Carson. If all is quiet at the end of the day, they will meet for dinner.

At 7.15 pm. Charmian decides to go and meet Biggs. She packs a bag with a few more shirts, and an electric razor that Biggs had forgotten in the rush to leave the house, plus some family photos.

As she tries to drive away from the house fourteen armed police surround Charmian in her car and raid the Biggs' house. Charmian is arrested and held at Fairlea Women's Prison before being transferred to Melbourne Police Watchhouse. Biggs leaves an unpaid bill of $3 and some clothes when he leaves the motel.

1969 - 20 October

Charmian is released from custody. Magistrates reject the Australian Immigration Department's request to hold her for seven days. She manages to sell her story to the Packer newspaper and television group for $A65,000, but only gets to keep A$25,000. The Australian tax authorities take the rest.

Biggs hides out in a house called Blue Waters, high up in the Dandenong Mountains that flank one side

of Melbourne. Biggs follows the search for him, and what is happening to his family, by listening to the radio.

1969 - 24 October

Biggs and Charmian are the cover of Private Eye. Eric Flower is arrested in the Beecroft suburb of Sydney, along with his wife and child.

Flower is arrested after a tip off that his wife had drawn out a large sum of money from a Sydney bank. Police believe the money is for Biggs.

1963 - 26 October

Following the news that Charmian has sold her story, an appeal fund is finally set up six years after the robbery for the driver Jack Mills. The belated public appeal raises £34,387 for Mills. About £460,000 at 2013 rates.

1969 - November

Alfie Gerrard, who helped Biggs and Flower in the UK after their escape, is tracked to Sydney and arrested. Biggs moves in with Mike and Jess Haynes. Mike offers Biggs his passport. Biggs uses his time with the Haynes to write down part of his story so far. It is 77 handwritten pages long.

1969 - 14 December

Eric Flower is returned to the UK and HMP Wandsworth.

1970 - January

Biggs gets to meet up with Charmian for the first time since being discovered in Australia. The meeting lasts for just one hour.

1970 - 9 January

The Australian police claim they have found two reels of 8mm film showing Biggs on holiday with his family in Spain. Biggs has never been to Spain. Charmian had been to Spain with other wives of the train robbers during the period between their conviction and the appeal.

1970 - 4 February

Train driver, Jack Mills, dies of lymphatic leukaemia. A coroner makes it clear that his death is in no way a result of what happened to him at the robbery.

1970 - 5 February
Biggs boards RHMS Ellinis in Melbourne as "Michael Haynes". Two days later, on 7 February, he leaves Australian waters after the ship sails from Sydney.

1970 - 21 February
The death of Jack Mills allows Peta Fordham, author of *The Robbers' Tale* and wife of one of the defence lawyers, to reveal the conversation she had with the driver.

She reveals it in a letter published in The Times. In it she says that Mills confirmed his main injury came from when he stumbled and hit his head on a ledge. Mills also told Fordham that his pension had been threatened if he had not made more during the trial and in interviews about the violence used towards him at the robbery.

1970 - 23 February
RHMS Ellinis docks in Panama. Three days later Biggs flies from Panama to Caracas. He leaves Caracas for Rio de Janeiro, Brazil, on 10 March.

1970 - 11 March
Ronnie Biggs lands in Rio de Janeiro and the city gains its most famous UK resident.

1970 - 20 April
Detective Chief Superintendent Tommy Butler, the Grey Fox, dies at the age of 57. Until the end he was looking for Biggs. Ironically on the same day as Butler's death, The Sun publishes Biggs' story - 'Ronald Biggs Talks' - which he had written while in hiding in Australia.

1970 - 26 June
The innocent William Boal dies in prison of a brain tumour. As Reynolds notes: "Boal was a victim of the judicial system."

1971 - 5 January
Biggs' eldest son, Nicholas, dies in a car crash in Melbourne, Australia. Police are out in force at the funeral looking for Biggs and remove all the cards from the flowers before Charmian has a chance to read them. Biggs will not learn of his son's death until a letter from Charmian reaches him in Rio in February.

1971 - March
To renew his visa; Biggs takes a side trip to Bolivia, not knowing he had chosen a well-watched drug route.

1971 - April
Roger Cordrey is the first of the main train robbery gang to be released from prison.

1971 - July
Biggs meets Raimunda de Castro, the mother to be of Mike Biggs, for the first time at the Bola Preta in Rio. Reynolds is moved from HMP Durham to HMP Chelmsford.

1972 - 6 January
Fireman David Whitby collapses and dies of a heart attack at his house in Crewe. He is 34.

1972
Sir Robert Mark, the Commissioner of the Met Police says: "I know only too well that there are a number of criminals active in London who are far more violent. It is only logical to wonder why... the Great Train Robbers should be regarded as qualifying for harsher treatment."

Reynolds is moved from HMP Chelmsford to HMP Leicester.

1973
Reynolds is moved from HMP Leicester to HMP Parkhurst on the Isle of White.

1973 - July
Detective Superintendent Frank Williams publishes *No Fixed Address: The Great Train Robbers on the Run*. In his book Williams blames the obsessive secretiveness of Tommy Butler for "at least three men" getting away with their part in the robbery. He also criticises the publishing of the photos of the robbers and their wives in the media.

1973 - November
Biggs talks with his friend Constantine Benckendorff about giving himself up. In December Benckendorff travels to London and meets with Colin Mackenzie of the Daily Express. Biggs sends Mackenzie a letter bearing his signature and a copy of his fingerprints.

The letter reads: 'Hi, Colin, Perhaps not the best set [of fingerprints] that have been taken, but certainly as good as those found on the Monopoly box and the sauce bottle! Convinced?! R.A. Biggs.'

1974 - 24 January

Colin Mackenzie and Daily Express news editor, Brian Hitchen, speak to Biggs by phone. He agrees to sell them his story. He will then fly back to the UK and give himself up to Scotland Yard.

1974 - 30 January

Mackenzie arrives in Rio. Biggs meets Mackenzie, Benckendorff and photographer Bill Lovelace in room 909 of the Trocadero Hotel in Copacabana. (Now the Arena Copacabana Hotel at Avenida Atlantica, 2064).

1974 - 1 February

Having been betrayed by the Daily Express, Biggs is surprised in the hotel room and arrested by Detective Chief Inspector Jack Slipper and Detective Inspector Peter Jones. Biggs is taken to the Federal Police Headquarters in the Catete Palace in Rio de Janeiro. Interviewed by Inspector Carlos Alberto Garcia, he decides that Biggs must be held over night while he consults with government authorities. Biggs, who knows that Raimunda is pregnant, learns for the first time that the father of a Brazilian child cannot be extradited.

1974 - 4 February

Furious that he has been double-crossed and not allowed to give himself up. Biggs decides to fight to stay in Brazil. Slipper and Jones return to London without Biggs. Papers from the archives released in 2005 reveal that the Foreign Office demanded that Scotland Yard apologise to Brazil's Federal Police. Biggs is never paid by the Express for his story.

1974 - 7 February

Biggs is transferred from Rio de Janeiro to a prison in the Brazilian capital, Brasilia. Neighbouring cellmate is the famous French forger Fernand Legros

1974 - 10 February

Charmian Biggs arrives in Brasilia to see Biggs.

1974 - 16 February

Biggs and Charmian are forced to 'hold' a press conference after the media are allowed into their private meeting. Biggs tells Charmian that he needs to divorce her so that he can marry Raimunda. Grenada Publishing offers Mackenzie a healthy advance for a book about Biggs.

1974 - March

Fernand Legros is deported back to France. Michael Haynes is prosecuted in Australia for helping Biggs. He serves time at Beechworth Prison, Victoria.

1974 - 6 May

A court orders that Biggs should be released and be 'deported', but not 'extradited'. This means finding another country without an extradition treaty with the UK. Biggs is transferred from Brasilia to Rio de Janeiro and 'released from custody'.

Biggs stays overnight at the Catete Palace, leaving on 7 May. Colin Mackenzie organises tickets for Charmian and the boys to visit Rio. Biggs moves into a rented apartment in Copacabana.

1974 - 16 May

Charmian, Chris and Farley Biggs arrive in Brazil and stay until 5 June.

1974 - 16 August

Michael Fernand Nascimento de Castro Biggs is born in Rio de Janeiro.

1974 – 8 November
Lord Lucan is suspected of murdering his children's nanny. He disappears. He replaces Biggs as the man the whole world is looking for.

1975
Colin Mackenzie publishes *The Most Wanted Man*. Raimunda is featured topless on the cover of News of the World with Biggs' new baby, Mike.

1975 - April
Buster Edwards and Jimmy White are released from prison in the same week. Edwards from HMP Wormwood Scrubs and White from HMP Gartree in Leicester. Edwards opens a flower stall close to Waterloo Station while White returns to his trade as a painter and decorator.

Edwards is interviewed by Piers Paul Read. He suggests to Read that he should write a book about the Great Train Robbery with the robbers.

1975 - 15 August
Roy James is the first of the "30 year" prisoners to be released. He is released from HMP Long Lartin, Worcestershire.

While in prison James has written to Graham Hill asking for his help when he comes out. At the time Hill was racing for Brabham, then owned by Bernie Ecclestone. Hill presents James to his team boss.

Roy James

Ecclestone says that he told James he was wasting his time because he had not been racing for over 10 years. James was also 37. But Ecclestone had heard that James was a very good silversmith so asked him to make a number of trophies to be used in Formula 1. Within weeks James breaks his leg at Abbey Corner while testing a car at Silverstone, and a "myth" begins that Ecclestone was involved in some way with the great Train Robbery, even as one of the three that got away or as the brains himself. Ecclestone has always treated the story in good humour, even being quoted as saying: "There wasn't enough money on that train!"

While in prison James had been asked by a fellow racing driver and friend, Rodney Banting, if he would make a trophy for the British Racing and Sports Car Club. Banting supplied the silver. The John Nicol Trophy, as it is known, is still presented annually by the BRSCC to a person for their contribution to motor racing.

1975 - 10 October
Buster Edwards is sent back to prison for six months for shop lifting £65.76 worth of goods from Harrods (about £400 worth in 2013 values).

1975 - November
Jim Hussey is released. The international press discover that Biggs is now living in Sepetiba, just outside of Rio. He starts doing press interviews for money.

1975 - December
Gordon Goody is released. He spends some time in the UK before moving to Spain where he buys and runs a bar, Kon-Tiki, in Mojacar.

1976 - February
Tommy Wisbey is released.

1976 - April
The media report that ten of the train robbers have formed themselves into a limited company to tell their own story of the train robbery. Three (Reynolds, Welch, Wilson) of the ten will be "sleeping partners" as they are still in prison. The company will also offer technical advice to anybody wishing to write or film any aspect of the robbery.

The Train Robbers - Buster, Wisbey, White, Reynolds, Cordrey, Wilson, Hussey

1976 - June
Bob Welch in released.

1976 - July
Gary van Dyk visits Rio de Janeiro to explain to Biggs the premise of Piers Paul Read's *The Train Robbers* and the "German" connection. The train robbers are to jointly write a book with Read for W.H.Allen.

Reynolds is moved from HMP Parkhurst to HMP Maidstone, in Kent. He is no longer a category A prisoner.

Ronnie Biggs and HMS Danae

1977 - February
Piers Paul Read visits Rio de Janeiro to talk with Biggs about the book and the German connection. He is shocked to hear from Biggs that part of it is not true. Later Read even suggests the "Germans" had visited Biggs in Rio to make him deny the connection.

1977 15-17 April
After Ronnie Biggs visits a Royal Naval warship in Rio de Janeiro, the HMS Danae, a diplomatic incident between Brazil and the UK is narrowly avoided.

1978 - February
Steve Jones and Paul Cook of the Sex Pistols, along with manager Malcolm McLaren, visit Brazil and Biggs. Biggs records and films with the Sex Pistols.

1978 - March
Piers Paul Read's *The Train Robbers* is published.

1978 - April
In preparation for his eventual parole and release, Reynolds is offered day release. He is moved to HMP Wormwood Scrubs, to a hostel that was formerly the gatehouse.

1978 - 28 May
Jimmy Hussey is expelled from West Germany for signing copies of *The Train Robbers*. This is due to Hussey having a previous conviction in Germany. Buster Edwards is allowed to stay.

1978 - 6 June
Bruce Reynolds is released from prison after serving ten years.

1978 - 8 June
Piers Paul Read and five of the train robbers address the Cambridge Union.

1978 - 30 June

Sex Pistols' *No One Is Innocent (A Punk Prayer)* is released with Biggs singing lead vocal. The song, the Sex Pistols' 5th single, goes to number six in the UK charts.

The death of Mary Manson.

1978 - 18 December

Charlie Wilson is the last of the imprisoned robbers to be released. Having spent most of his sentence in HMP Parkhurst, he is released from HMP Pentonville in London.

Buster Edwards

1979 - February

British Leyland poster and ad campaign for the Mini bears the legend: 'Nips In & Out Like Ronald Biggs'. One of the posters is in front of Buster's stall at Waterloo Station. Ironically the Advertising Standards Authority accuses British Leyland of not asking Biggs if they could use his name.

1979 - April

A kidnap attempt on Biggs in Rio by John Miller, Fred Prime and Norman ("Norrie") Boyle is thwarted. The men pretend to be linked to the film crew shooting James Bond's *Moonraker* and try to get Biggs to fly to the set of the film for a cameo role in the film. UK journalists, who have heard rumours of the plot to kidnap him, tip Biggs off. The men are expelled from Brazil, but are not charged.

1979 - 28 April

Brian Field, the link to the 'Ulsterman', dies in a car crash with his new wife, Sian. He had changed his name to Brian Carlton on release, and been involved with the book trade. The car crash is caused by a car being driven by the daughter of celebrity hairdresser Teasy Weasy Raymon ("Bessone") crossing the M4 barrier and hitting Field's car head on.

1980 - 15 May

Premier of the Sex Pistols' *The Great Rock & Roll Swindle*, a film directed by Julien Temple that features the band with Ronnie Biggs.

While on the run, Alfie Gerrard dies in Brighton from an internal haemorrhage.

1981

Detective Chief Superintendent Jack Slipper publishes his autobiography *Slipper of the Yard*. "I think the public saw the situation between Biggs and me as a good cops and robbers story", he says. "But there was never any personal animosity between the two of us. Like most professional villains, Ronnie respects a good, fair copper, and I have to admire him, too. I got on very well with Ronnie and we never had a crossword. But now I only have sympathy for him."

1981 - 9 March

Biggs agrees to be interviewed in Rio by Patrick King for National Geographic

Biggs and John Miller

1981 - 16 March

Biggs is kidnapped from the Roda Viva restaurant in Rio where he has gone to meet King. He is bundled into a bag and flown by a private plane from Rio to Belem and put on the yacht Nowcani II. He is told to cooperate or they will kill his son, Mike. John Miller, Fred Prime, Mark Algate, Anthony Marriage, Thorfinn Maciver and Patrick King are the kidnappers. John Miller, an ex-Scot's Guard, will say that Sir Hugh Fraser, who then owned Harrods, financed the kidnapping of Biggs. At first there is speculation that Biggs' disappearance is a publicity stunt. Kidnappers ask the UK media for £500,000 for Biggs.

1981 - 24 March
Biggs is landed in Barbados after the Nowcani II breaks down. He is arrested but his kidnappers are allowed to go free and encouraged to leave the island.

1981 - 25 March
Ezra Alleyne 'Sunshine', who would be his lawyer in Barbados along with Frederick Smith, visits Biggs for the first time. By fate Ezra had worked in London for Ellis Lincoln, the solicitor who had handled the defences of Wisbey, Welch and Hussey. Ezra had been a regular presence at the original trial as part of the Lincoln legal team.

Ezra tells Biggs: 'Mr Lincoln taught me something that I will never forget. It doesn't matter how difficult a case may appear to be - there is always a loophole. And, if you will allow me, I would like to find the loophole that will enable you to return to Brazil.'

1981 - 5 April
Biggs' first hearing before a magistrates' court in Barbados. Biggs, will be sent back to the UK.

1981 - 23 April
An appeal hearing takes place in front of two judges from the Barbados High Court. Barbados Chief Justice Sir William Douglas and Deputy Chief Justice Denys Williams.

1981 - 24 April
Biggs' case is dismissed after the prosecution is shown to have made some serious legal errors in its case. Biggs is a free man and returns to Rio de Janeiro from Barbados forty days after being kidnapped. He flies by a private jet paid for by ITV and Brazil's TV Globo.

1981 - May
As part of the deal with Murdoch to pay Biggs' lawyers, Charmian with Farley visits Biggs in Rio.

They stay for just four days. Charmian says Biggs was more interested in signing autographs than talking to her.

While Biggs had been kidnapped his son Mike has appeared on Brazilian TV pleading for his father's return. This not only mobilised the Brazilian Government, but Mike was also spotted by the head of CBS Records in Brazil who saw potential star quality in Mike. A new kids' band is born, A Turma do Balão Magico (Magic Balloon Gang), with Mike Biggs, Simony and Toby.

1982 - 22 March
Tommy Wisbey is fined £500 for handling stolen travellers cheques taken from a mail train.

1982 - June
Biggs starts selling his "I know someone who went to Brazil and met Ronnie Biggs... honest!" t-shirt.

Sting and Biggs

1983 - 17 February
The Police finally catch up with Ronnie Biggs in Rio. But this is the group fronted by Sting.

1983 - 26 November
Brink's-Matt robbery takes place at London Heathrow Airport. £26 million worth of gold, diamonds and cash is stolen. It is the largest robbery in the UK since the Great Train Robbery. Charlie Wilson is later suspected of laundering some of the proceeds for the gang.

1984 - February
Biggs buys an apartment for Mike at 470 Rua Monte

Alegre in Santa Teresa from the proceeds of A Turma do Balão Magico's record sales, TV series and live shows. The band sells over 10 million albums and is the 20th most successful Brazilian acts of all time.

The flat in Santa Teresa will be Biggs' home in Rio until he returns to the UK. Biggs also films 'Long time No See Ronnie' for Japanese television.

1984 - 10 February
Roy James marries 18-year-old Anthea Wadlow in Croydon.

1984 - 9 March
Patricia Wilson, wife of Charlie Wilson, goes to court to try and unblock her bank account. The Inland Revenue are asking her to explain £180,000 in the account (about £480,000 in 2013 values).

1984 - April
Diesel engine D326, the engine involved in the Great Train Robbery, is withdrawn from service in February and cut up for scrap in April.

Charlie Wilson, Roy James and four others are in court accused of a £2.4 million VAT fraud involving gold coins. James is acquitted. Wilson pays £400,000 to HMRC to avoid a retrial.

1984 - June
Linslade Court House, built in the 19th century, is to be sold after a new magistrates court is opened in Aylesbury. The building is subsequently converted into flats.

1984 - October
Bruce Reynolds is sent back to prison for three years for handling amphetamine sulphate. A charge he has always denied.

1985 - March
Bruce Reynolds is released from prison. His friend Terry Hogan offers him a job.

Charlie Wilson is arrested and accused of taking part in the armed robbery of a security van.

He spends four months in jail, but the charges are dropped following allegations of police corruption.

1985 - 25 April
Paul Hardcastle, who had a number one hit with *19*, releases *Just For the Money* which goes to number 19 in the UK chart. With a large section of the song about the Great Train Robbery, the song and video include performances by Sir Laurence Olivier and Bob Hoskins.

1985 - July
Biggs holds a party to celebrate 20 years on the run. Charmian, his first wife; Raimunda, mother of Mike; and Ulla, his partner in Brazil, are all present.

Biggs and Lech Majewski

1986-87
Biggs meets Polish film director Lech Majewski who he is introduced to by Freddie Foreman. Biggs and Majewski start work on the screenplay for *Prisoner of Rio* that is meant to be the true story of what has happened to Biggs in Rio. Majewski changes his mind and decides to turn to fiction and write another kidnap story. The kidnap to be carried out by an outraged Scotland Yard Inspector, 'Jock' McFarland, who is obsessed with the idea of getting 'that bastard' out of Brazil. It starts filming in Rio in July 1987 after being announced at the Cannes Film Festival by Mike Biggs in May 1987. Mike also visits London and meets with Buster Edwards. The cast of *Prisoner of Rio* includes Steven Berkoff, Peter Firth, Desmond Llewelyn and Paul Freeman as Biggs.

Producer Norma Heyman with
Ralph Brown, Michael Attwell,
Larry Lamb and Phil Collins

1988 - February

Charmian visits Biggs in Rio along with Chris and Farley. Biggs shows them carnival before Charmian goes off to visit Peru and Bolivia. Farley celebrates his 21st birthday in Rio on 21 April with Biggs, Charmian and Chris.

1988 - 12 May

Prisoner of Rio is screened at the Cannes Film Festival. It is not well received by critics or buyers. Charlie Wilson moves to Spain.

1988 - 8 August - 25th Anniversary of the Great Train Robbery

Virgin Books publish *Biggsy's Bible: The World's Most Wanted Book*. It includes sections on how to bring up your child as a criminal and how to get rich quick.

1988 - 15 September

The world premiere of *Buster* takes place at the Odeon Leicester Square. Produced by Norma Heyman, the mother of 'Harry Potter' producer David Heyman. It is directed by David Green and stars Phil Collins and Julie Walters. Larry Lamb plays Bruce Reynolds.

The film is to be a Royal Premiere with the Prince and Princess of Wales in attendance to raise money for the Prince's Trust, but a campaign lead by Alexander Walker of the Evening Standard leads to the cancellation of the royal couple. The premiere still raises over £100,000 for the Prince's Trust.

1988 - 11 November

BBC TV screens *The Great Paper Chase*, based on Anthony Delano's book *Slip-Up*. In 1990 Jack Slipper is awarded £50,000 in damages for libel from the BBC.

1989 - 26 July

Tommy Wisbey and Jimmy Hussey plead guilty and are convicted for trafficking cocaine worth over £500,000. They are sentenced to 10 and 7 years respectively. Hussey is caught with the drugs on

him, while a supply is also found at Wisbey's home after the police had seen him passing the package to Hussey.

1990 - 24 April

Charlie Wilson is found murdered at his villa in Marbella on Spain's Costa del Sol. His dog is killed with him.

1990 - 10 May

Charlie Wilson's funeral in the UK. Bruce Reynolds, Buster Edwards, Bob Welch and Roy James all attend.

1990 - July

Paul Seabourne, who was the key figure in helping Biggs to escape from HMP Wandsworth, visits Biggs in Rio.

1990 - 27 July

An arrest Warrant is issued for Biggs at Bow Street Magistrates Court. The same document will be used hen he returns to the UK in 2001.

1990 - 28 September

Roy Atkins, the man thought to have ordered the killing of Charlie Wilson, is gunned down in the Nightwatch bar of the American Hotel in Amsterdam.

1991 - January

In Rio de Janeiro to perform at Rock in Rio 2 in the Maracana stadium, the Happy Mondays visit Biggs accompanied by Piers Morgan who is covering the festival for The Sun.

Bruce, Nick, Mike and Ronnie

1991 - March

Steven Berkoff publishes *A Prisoner in Rio*, his account of making the film and meeting Biggs.

1991 - April

Princess Diana, the Princess of Wales, visits Rio with Prince Charles. The British press want Biggs to meet Diana, but he declines. Reynolds and his son Nick also visit Biggs in Rio. It is the first time Reynolds and Biggs have met since the robbery.

1991 - June

Actor Dexter Fletcher steals two bunches of flowers valued at £5 from Buster Edwards' flower stall. Edwards reports the incident to the police and can name Fletcher as he has just seen him in the film *The Rachel Papers*. Fletcher is arrested, charged, and pleads guilty. He later apologises to Edwards.

The German rock band, Die Toten Hosen, visit Biggs in Rio and record *Carnival in Rio (Punk Was)* and *Police on My Back* with him. It is the start of a long friendship and collaboration.

1992 - August

The owner of Leatherslade Farm, Paul Morris, applies for permission to demolish the farm and rebuild it.

1992 - 26 December

Lord Edmund Davies, the judge at the Great Train Robbery trial, dies.

1993 – 6 May

Roy James is arrested for shooting his ex-father-in-law, David Wadlow, three times and pistol whipping his ex-wife, Anthea James, who he divorced in 1990. His eight-year-old daughter talks James in to putting the gun, a Second World War revolver, down. He is sentenced to six years in January 1994.

June 1993

Jack Slipper visits Biggs in Rio de Janeiro for the Sunday Express. He asks Biggs to name the three that got away. Biggs declines. Biggs once receive an offer of "one million dollars" to name the three.

1994 - 21 January

Biggs publishes his autobiography, *Odd Man Out*.

A best seller for pre-Harry Potter Bloomsbury publishing.

1994 - 29 November
Buster Edwards is found hanged in his lock up on the corner of Greet Street and Brad Street, close to Waterloo Station, where he stores the barrow and stall for the flower business he had run for 20 years. A number of theories are put forward as to why he committed suicide. Some people believe he did not.

1994 - 9 December
Buster Edwards' funeral. Bruce Reynolds, Bob Welch and Tommy Wisbey attend. Freddie Foreman is told he may not attend as he is out of prison on licence. He hides in the crowd by Buster's flower stall to pay his respects.

1995 - 15 January
Terry Hogan, a very close friend of Reynolds, who was often suspected of being one of the three train robbers who was never caught, commits suicide. He was in Cannes on the day of the robbery.

1995 - 5 February
Biggs is a guest of the Rolling Stones for their Voodoo Lounge show at the Maracana Stadium. Having met the Stones, Biggs watches the show with Keith Richards' father.

1995 - February
Biggs breaks his leg after a fall in Rio. Uri Geller visits Rio and Biggs asks him to heal his leg!

1995 - April
Bruce Reynolds publishes *Autobiography of a Thief* to much acclaim.

1995 - 18 July
The UK and Brazilian Foreign Secretaries, Malcolm Rifkind and Luiz Felipe Lamprea, sign a new extradition treaty between the UK and Brazil.

1995 - August
Nick Reynolds flies to Rio to do a cast of Biggs for his 'Heroes & Villains' and 'Cons to Icons' collections. Roy "Pretty Boy" Shaw is also there.

1995 - 31 October
After the success of *Odd Man Out*, Biggs writes a novel with his 'ghost', Chris Pickard.

Keep On Running, published by Bloomsbury, is loosely based on the 'Ulsterman' and the three train robbers who got away and were never charged. Some papers take it to be the truth, including that packages of South African diamonds were on the train.

1996 - 21 July
Assistant Chief Constable Gerard McArthur dies.

1996 - October
Roy James undergoes triple bypass surgery in prison. He is released in early 1967.

1997 - 14 August
New extradition treaty between Brazil and UK becomes law.

1997 - 20 August
Roy James dies of a heart attack in the Brompton Hospital at the age of 62.

Danny Roff, the man thought to have shot Charlie Wilson, is gunned down at his home in Bromley, south London. 18 months earlier he had been shot in the back in a nightclub in New Cross, south London, since when Ruff has been confined to a wheelchair.

1997 - 29 October

Foreign Secretary Jack Straw officially asks Brazil to extradite Biggs. On 12 November, Brazil's Supreme Court rejects the request. The court rules that the statute of limitations has run out on the robbery, as the crime was committed more than 20 years ago and Biggs has committed no crimes in Brazil.

1998 - February

Unidos do Porto da Pedra samba school honours Biggs at Rio's carnival with *Samba no pé e mãos ao alto, isto é um assalto (Stick 'em up, put your hands in the air and samba on your feet.)* It is a very rare honour for non-Brazilians to be the theme of a major samba school's parade.

1998 - 16 March

Biggs suffers a stroke. He is treated at the São Silvestre Hospital. Following the stroke Biggs is temporarily unable to speak. Charmian visits Rio to help Biggs with his recovery.

1998 - December

Roy 'Pretty Boy' Shaw visits Biggs for Christmas in Rio.

1999 - May

Bruce Reynolds addresses the pupils at Eton.

Biggs and Reynolds, Ron's 70th

Happy Birthday
70
Ronald Biggs

1999 - 8 August

Biggs' 70th Birthday Celebrations. Bruce Reynolds and his son Nick join Biggs in Rio. Others attending from the UK include Roy Shaw, Tony Hoare and Dave Courtney. In total more than 150 guests attend the party. Invitations to the party are printed on the back of a £5 Monopoly note.

1999 - 10 August

Secret History - The Great Train Robbery is broadcast on Channel 4.

1999 - 15 September

Biggs suffers a second stroke. A week later, on 22 September, he suffers a third and far more serious stroke that leaves him without speech.

One of Biggs first visitors after his stroke is Steven Berkoff who notes: "The loss of his speech is a painful blow for a born gabber and a man who, as Hamlet says of Yorick, 'could set the table on a road.'"

1999 - October

SCi, a games manufacturer famous for *Carmaggeddon*, to support a game based on the Great Train Robbery, approaches Reynolds and Biggs.

1999 - November

Debilitated by his strokes, Biggs attempts suicide. He is saved by his son, Mike.

2000 - 9 June

Gangster Number 1, starring Malcolm McDowell, David Thewlis, Paul Bettany and Jamie Foreman, opens in London. Script advice comes from Reynolds and Freddie Foreman.

2001 - 8 March

First contact is made with 'The Sun' about Biggs' possible return to the UK from Brazil. On 16 March Mike Biggs visits The Sun with Nick Reynolds. They meet with Graham Dudman, The Sun's Assistant News Editor, and the Crime Editor Mike Sullivan

2001 - 6 April

Mike Sullivan and John Askill of The Sun fly to Rio to meet Biggs. An initial deal is struck and negotiated

for Biggs' return. A mid-May date considered.

2001 - 1 May
The Sun moves the date of Biggs return forward as it fears that other papers have got hold of the story. Mike Sullivan briefs John Coles, head of the Flying Squad.

2001 - 2 May
Biggs emails John Coles at Scotland Yard to say he wants to return: 'I would like to give myself up to you. What I need is passport documentation to travel back to Britain. I am prepared to be arrested at the gate when I arrive at Heathrow airport and submit myself to the due process of the law.'

2001 - 3 May
News of Biggs' imminent return breaks in the global media. The Sun's editor, David Yelland, calls the Foreign Secretary about Biggs' need for a passport.

2001 - 4 May
The Sun's private plane, leased from TAG Aviation, departs from Farnborough at 3.07 pm to Rio. Bruce and Nick Reynolds are on board as guests of honour.

2001 - 5 May
Biggs is reunited with Bruce and Nick Reynolds.

2001 - 6 May
Biggs receives an Emergency British Passport (E.P.196182). His first ever-genuine passport. He leaves Brazil on The Sun's private plane that takes off from Rio's International Airport at 5.18 pm local time (9.18 pm in London). Bruce and Nick Reynolds are on board, as well as Ron's son Mike.

2001 - 7 May
Biggs returns to the UK landing at RAF Northolt at 8.47 am. Biggs has been on the run for 13,068 days. He is arrested by Detective Chief Superintendent John Coles, charged and transferred to the hospital wing of HMP Belmarsh, Britain's highest security prison, via Chiswick Police Station and the West London Courthouse. With 28 years of his sentence still to serve, Biggs is given his old prison number from Wandsworth: 002731.

Biggs and the Great Train Robbery have dominated the cover of The Sun for a week.

2001 - 2 June
Biggs collapses in HMP Belmarsh and is rushed to Queen Elizabeth Hospital following a fourth stroke. He is handcuffed to his bed.

2001 - 21 July
Biggs meets Lord Jeffrey Archer in HMP Belmarsh.

2002 - 30 January

Criminal Cases Review Commission rejects an application to send Biggs' case to the Court of Appeal.

2002 - 31 January

A two-hour, two-part documentary, *The Legend of Ronnie Biggs*, airs on Channel Five in the UK.

2002 - 10 July

Biggs marries Mike's mother, Raimunda Rothen at Belmarsh in front of 11 guests. The reception (without Biggs) is held in the Punch Bowl pub in Mayfair owned by Freddie Foreman's son, Greg.

2002 - 24 July

Mike Biggs is granted British citizenship following the marriage of Biggs and Raimunda. Mike and Veronica, mother of Biggs granddaughter, Ingrid, wed.

2003- 2 October

A High Court judge throws out Biggs' appeal against his sentence. The judge calls the appeal 'hopeless' and 'misconceived'.

2004 - 6 January

A suspected heart attack sees Biggs return to Queen Elizabeth Hospital. In August he is rushed to Queen Elizabeth Hospital for a fifth time.

2005 - 14 March

The 60-minute documentary *Ronnie Biggs: Last Escape?* airs on Sky One in the UK. Giovanni di Stefano becomes Biggs' lawyer.

2005 - 24 August

After a long illness, Jack Slipper dies at the age of 81. Biggs asks permission to go to the funeral, but is refused.

2005 - 11 October

Channel 4 airs *Kidnap Ronnie Biggs* in the UK despite Biggs' protest to the channel that it is factually inaccurate and produced by the kidnappers.

2005 - 28 November

Detective Superintendent Malcolm Fewtrell dies.

2007 - 4 July

Biggs is transferred from HMP Belmarsh to HMP Norwich on "compassionate grounds". Biggs has been held in Belmarsh for nearly 74 months.

Biggs is pleased to see that the roof he built at Norwich in 1958 is still standing.

2008 - 21 July

Robbery, starring Stanley Baker and directed by Peter Yates, is finally released on DVD in the UK.

2008 - 16 October

Harry Smith, one of the key suspects of the robbery never to be charged, dies. Death certificate lists his occupation as a retired property consultant.

2009 - 17 February

Mark Leech, the editor of *The Prisons Handbook*, says Justice Secretary Jack Straw tells him: "The problem with Mr Biggs is no-one has formally asked me for his release."

2009 – March

Papers submitted by Giovanni di Stefano for Biggs' parole under the discretionary Release Scheme. Biggs' health deteriorates.

2009 - 23 April

Biggs applies for parole. He is eligible for release on 3 July 2009 after he has served one-third of his sentence. The decision is delayed while arrangements are made as to who will pay for the 24-hour care that Biggs will require.

2009 - 15 June

The Parole Board recommends to Justice Secretary Jack Straw that Biggs be released; saying the risk of him reoffending is "manageable".

2009 - 28 June

Biggs is taken to Norfolk & Norwich University Hospital with a suspected broken hip and a chest infection.

2009 - 1 July

While Biggs is in hospital he is refused parole by the Justice Secretary Jack Straw who says Biggs is "wholly unrepentant".

A BITTER END

1963 ▲ **IN THE DOCK** Train robber Biggs in a suit for the trial and, right, being marched into court at Aylesbury by a policeman

1969 ▲ **WANTED MAN** Face of a fugitive

1979 ▲ **ON THE RUN** With his son Michael in Brazil where he lived for three decades

BY **DAVID COLLINS**
d.collins@mirror.co.uk

Freed Biggs 'not going to the pub, not going to Rio, he's going to die'

DYING Ronnie Biggs was last night told he is a free man.

But the Great Train Robber will not be getting his last wish of a pint down the pub.

Justice secretary Jack Straw released him him on compassionate grounds. But the fugitive who led Scotland Yard on a chase around the world has severe pneumonia and is not expected to live beyond the weekend.

He will be 80 tomorrow – the 46th anniversary of the robbery that catapulted him to notoriety.

His legal adviser, Giovanni Di Stefano, said: "He is being let out to die and that cannot be considered a victory. But it's a victory for common sense. This man is ill, he's going to die, he is not going to any pub or going to Rio, he is going to stay in hospital."

Son Michael said: "I'm delighted. Finally common sense has prevailed. I hope my father can survive to enjoy his birthday and whatever time he's got left."

If Biggs rallies he hopes to move him from hospital to a nursing home in Barnet, North London, for his final days. Mr Straw said the release was based on medical evidence Biggs was not expected to recover. Only last month he rejected parole on the grounds he was "wholly unrepentant" .

He said yesterday: "Medical evidence clearly shows Mr Biggs is very ill and that his condition has deteriorated recently. It is not expected to improve."

Biggs – who has had a series of strokes, is fed by tube and can only communicate by blinking – was rushed to Norwich and Norfolk Hospital from his cell at Norwich on Tuesday.

Mike Gray, who wrote a biography of the robber and was one of the first to learn of the release, said: "It's better for all now if Ronnie dies. He's very, very ill."

The three prison staff watching him will leave today once the release licence is finalised.

Biggs, from Lambeth, South London, was one of a 15-strong gang which attacked a mail train at Ledburn, Bucks, in 1963 and stole £2.6million in used notes.

He was given 30 years but after 15 months escaped from Wandsworth by climbing a 30ft wall and fleeing in a furniture van.

Biggs was on the run for more than 30 years, living in Australia and fathering son Michael in Brazil before returning in 2001 in search of medical treatment.

When he landed he said his last wish was to buy a pint of bitter in a pub in Margate.

The son of Jack Mills, the driver clubbed around the head in the Great Train Robbery, yesterday refused to comment on news the release. John Mills said: "I don't wish to talk about this."

1992 ▲ **LIFE OF RILEY** Relaxing in Rio

2000 ▲ **FREE MAN** In Brazil after escaping extradition to UK

2005 ▲ **FRAIL** He comes back to England for healthcare

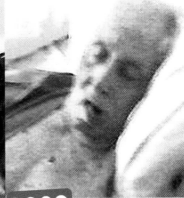

2009 ▲ **BARELY ALIVE** Sleeping on hospital bed awaiting pardon

WHATEVER HAPPENED TO THE GREAT TRAIN ROBBERS?

BRUCE REYNOLDS: Nicknamed "Napoleon", he masterminded the robbery. He fled to Mexico and then Canada, returning to England when the loot ran out. In 1968, he was apprehended in Torquay and got 25 years in jail.

Released in 1978, he moved into a cramped flat off London's Edgware Road. In the 80s he was jailed for three years for dealing amphetamines. In his 1995 memoirs he said the robbery was a curse: "I became an old crook living on handouts from other old crooks."

RONALD 'BUSTER' EDWARDS: Fled to Mexico but gave himself up in 1966. Believed to have wielded the cosh on train driver Jack Mills. Edwards served nine years, then sold flowers outside London's Waterloo Station. Found hanged in a garage in 1994, aged 62.

CHARLIE WILSON: The gang's treasurer. Jailed for 30 years in 1964, he escaped after four months. Caught in Canada after four years on the run and served 10 more years. Released in 1978, he moved to Marbella. Shot dead by a hitman in 1990.

TOMMY WISBEY: Released in 1976 but jailed for 10 more years in 1989 for drug dealing. Now residing in North London.

BOBBY WELCH: Released in 1976, he became a car dealer in London. Left crippled after surgery on his leg went wrong.

GORDON GOODY: After his 1975 release, he ran a bar in Spain.

▲ **GANG** (l to r) Reynolds, Edwards, Wilson, Wisbey, Welch, Goody and, left, part of haul

2009 - 17 July
Biggs is transferred from hospital back to HMP Norwich. A Judicial Review is submitted.

2009 - 28 July
Biggs is rushed back to Norfolk & Norwich University Hospital with severe pneumonia. Mike Biggs is told to go urgently to the hospital. A request is made for clemency.

2009 - 30 July
A Judicial Review is granted by the High Court for Biggs' right for parole.

2009 - 6 August
Justice Secretary Jack Straw announces that he will free Biggs on compassionate grounds. It is a Thursday. The same Thursday that 46 years earlier, in 1963, had been the day of the Great Train Robbery.

2009 - 7 August
Ronald Biggs, the last of the train robbers in prison, is released. He has served 3,875 days for his part in the Great Train Robbery out of a sentence of 10,957 days. He has also spent 13,068 days on the run.

2009 - 17 August
Biggs is transferred from Norfolk & Norwich University Hospital to a nursing home in Barnet.

2010 – 19 August
Signal Red, a fictional novel by Robert Ryan based on The Great Train Robbery is published. It is part used as the basis for the BBC series in 2013.

2010 - 30 December
Death of Frances 'Angela' Reynolds.

2011 - 14 February
Giovanni di Stefano is arrested in Majorca on a European Arrest Warrant. The warrant is issued 'on matters relating to fraud, theft and money laundering.'

2011 - July
Papers released by the National Archives show that The Sun newspaper sought advice in 1970 from Scotland Yard regarding the authenticity of a Biggs manuscript. A lawyer representing Charmian offered the 77-page manuscript to the paper in Australia.

2011 - 17 November
Biggs publishes his final updated autobiography, *Ronnie Biggs - Odd Man Out: The Last Straw*. It is launched at Shoreditch House in East London where he gives his first press conference in the UK. Mike Biggs and Nick Reynolds are there to support him.

2012 – September-October
ITV airs the five part series *Mrs Biggs* starring Daniel Mays as Biggs and Sheridan Smith as Charmian. Despite claiming to be the 'true story' it is full of factual errors and dramatic licence – the producer's ignoring Biggs offer to check the facts. It is screened in Australia in April 2013

2012 - 12 November
Jimmy Hussey dies in St Christopher's Hospice in Sydenham. Somebody calls The Sun and says that on his deathbed Jimmy Hussey confessed that it was him who coshed Jack Mills. It was not.

Jimmy White, living as James Patten, dies.

2013 - 1 January
Ronnie Biggs is back at number one on the Death List (www.deathlist.net). His 13th appearance on the list. Andrew Cook publishes 'The Great Train Robbery: The Untold Story from the Closed Investigation Files.'

2013 – 9 January
Based on Andrew Cook's book, 'The Great Train Robbery's Missing Mastermind?' airs on Channel 4.

2013 - 28 February
Bruce Reynolds dies in his sleep at his home in Croydon. His son Nick is with him.

2013 - 20 March
The funeral of Bruce Reynolds is held at St Bartholomew the Great, Smithfield, London. Biggs and Bob Welch attend the funeral.

John Daly is not well enough to attend and Gordon Goody, who sends a note to be read at the service, is

MR BIG OF GREAT TRAIN ROBBERY

NICKED Reynolds in cuffs after return to UK

'Mastermind' Reynolds dies in sleep at 81

BY BEN ROSSINGTON
ben.rossington@trinitymirror.com

THE brains behind the Great Train Robbery died yesterday aged 81.

Bruce Reynolds led the 17-strong gang that escaped with £2.6million in used notes in 1963 – the equivalent of £41million today.

Fellow gang member Ronnie Biggs, 83, wept when he was told the news.

Son Michael, 38, said: "My father showed a lot of emotion and there were tears. Bruce was his oldest friend – someone he had known since they met in borstal when he was 13."

Reynold's artist son Nick, a member of the band Alabama 3 who recorded the theme tunes to TV gangster series The Sopranos, confirmed his dad had died in his sleep at home in Croydon, South London. He called him "a quintessential Englishman who spent some time on the wrong side of the tracks".

Eddie Richardson, the 1960s London gang boss, said: "He was his own man. He done his own thing. There's only a couple left now."

HISTORY

Former antiques dealer Reynolds, nick-named Napoleon, wanted to pull off a crime to go down in history. At just after 3am on August 8, 1963, driver Jack Mills stopped his mail train at a red light at Ledburn, Bucks.

The gang, who had rigged the lights, coshed Mills, handcuffed him to his mate and helped themselves to the loot.

Reynolds fled to Mexico and was joined by his wife and son but the cash soon ran out and he came back to England. In 1968 he was found in Torquay and sentenced to 25 years.

Paroled in 1978 he moved, alone and penni-less, to a tiny London flat. In the 80s he got three years for dealing amphetamines.

Most of the train cash was never recovered but 13 men were jailed with many getting 30-year terms although all served less.

Biggs, a fugitive for 36 years, returned in 2001 and was freed from jail due to illness.

Last night Reynolds' family friend John Schoonraad said Bruce turned his back on crime in later life. He added "He did his time and turned into a very nice man."

ON RUN Police pic of Reynolds and wife

FOUND Mirror after arrest

ICON Artist son Nick made bronze cast of Reynolds

KEY GANG MEMBERS.. THE COP AND THE VICTIM

RONNIE BIGGS
NOW 83. Broke out of jail in 1965 and went to Brazil. Returned to UK in 2001

BUSTER EDWARDS
FLED to Mexico, but later served nine years. Found hanged in 1994 aged 62

CHARLIE WILSON
GANG treasurer, escaped from jail but did 10 years. Killed by a hitman in 1990

JIMMY HUSSEY
CONFESSED on his death bed last year aged 79 that he had coshed the driver

JACK SLIPPER
GIVEN job of finding the robbers. Tracked Biggs to Brazil. Died 1999 aged 81.

JACK MILLS
DRIVER hit with iron bar. He never fully recovered. Died of cancer aged 64.

not well enough to fly to London from Spain. Nick Reynolds's band, Alabama 3, perform *Too Sick To Pray*.

2013 - 27 March
Giovanni di Stefano, Biggs' lawyer, is convicted on 25 charges, including deception, fraud and money laundering between 2001 and 2011. He is sentenced to 14 years.

The judge describes Di Stefano's crimes as "planned and persistent," and his overall conduct as showing "greed, dishonesty and utter disregard for the sensibilities of others."

2013 - 10 April
The death of John Daly from a rare disease that has led to multiple organ failure.

He lived in Launceston, in east Cornwell, and none of his neighbours knew of his past.

2013 - 8 August
The 50th Anniversary of the Great Train Robbery and the 84th birthday of Ronnie Biggs.

The BBC commissions two films to mark the 50th anniversary of the robbery. *A Robber's Tale*, directed by Julian Jarrold, tells the story of the gang. The cast includes Luke Evans (Reynolds), Jack Roth (Wilson), Neil Maskell (Buster), Paul Anderson (Goody), Martin Compston (James), Del Synnott (Brian Field) and Jack Gordon (Biggs).

Film two is *A Copper's Tale*, directed by James Strong, that tells the story of Tommy Butler and his team of detectives. Jim Broadbent plays Butler.

Gordon Goody agrees to be interviewed for a new documentary to be directed by Chris Long, executive producer of *The Mentalist*.

Ronnie Biggs releases the Kindle version of *Keep On Running*.

If you want to read in more detail about the fascinating lives and times of Bruce Reynolds and Ronnie Biggs, both of whom contributed greatly to this publication, make sure you read their own autobiographies, respectively *The Autobiography of a Thief* and *Odd Man Out: The Last Straw*.

"Dreaming of El Dorado"

Bronze of Bruce Reynolds
by his son, Nick Reynolds

Bruce Reynolds
The final words

Friends old and young attended the funeral of Bruce Reynolds on Wednesday 20 March 2013. Duncan Campbell, who had met and interviewed Bruce on a number of occasions, covered the event for The Guardian. This is his report.

The church of St Bartholomew the Great in Smithfield, just round the corner from the Old Bailey, has seen everything in its 900-year history, from the Great Fire of London to the bombs of the second world war.

But it can never have hosted an event quite like this. The occasion was the funeral of Bruce Richard Reynolds, ringleader of the Great Train Robbery that took place almost exactly 50 years ago.

Many of his fellow robbers have already had their collars felt by the almighty but perhaps the best known of them, Ronnie Biggs, now partially paralysed through a series of strokes, was in attendance. He gave a cheery two fingers to the massed ranks of photographers as he arrived.

Unable to speak now, Biggs had a message read out on his behalf: "Bruce was a true friend, a friend through good and bad times and we had plenty of

both." Another of the old robbers, Bob Welsh, was there too, also in a wheelchair.

"I come to bury Caesar, not to praise him," said the Rev Martin Dudley, the church's rector, as he opened the ceremony. "A man is not defined by one act. There is always the bigger picture." And over the next hour and a half, a portrait of the man who planned what became Britain's most famous robbery was painted in bright colours.

The funeral was organised by Reynolds' son, Nick, who was a diver with the Royal Navy during the Falklands war and is now a sculptor and a musician with the Alabama 3, creators of the theme tune of The Sopranos.

He had wanted to get away from the old-style gangster's send-off, so there was to be no floral tribute in the shape of a mailbag, no playing of Frank Sinatra's version of My Way. Instead, there were tales from friends, music from the band and the church's own magnificent choir.

Nick Reynolds described his father as "my best friend, soulmate and older brother ... He chose a lunatic path and paid the price."

He recounted how his father had studied sociology in prison under the tutelage of Professor Laurie Taylor and the late Stan Cohen and had become a different person.

"He was an artist at heart and although he referred to the train robbery as his Sistine Chapel, his greatest triumph was in reassessing himself and changing his attitude about what was important in life."

Of the looming August anniversary of the robbery, he said his father had not been looking forward to all the bother from the media. "So, as he had so often done before when wanted for questioning, he chose to split the scene." Nick's sons, Spiggy and Otto, read poems for their grandfather.

The actor David Thewlis, who met Reynolds while making the film Gangster Number One, said there had always been a great affinity between actors and thieves as each needed the skills of the other "Thieves are, by necessity, great actors," he said. Thewlis described his conversations with Reynolds in the eccentric Clerkenwell watering hole The Tardis, "about Jesse James and James Joyce".

The writer Jake Arnott recalled that on his meeting with Reynolds, the latter had quoted William Burroughs: "Steal everything in sight." He praised his writing, describing Reynolds' memoirs, The Autobiography of a Thief, as a modern classic. "His life was like a novel. Bruce knew more than most about the need for adventure."

The instantly recognisable punk poet John Cooper Clark had been prompted by news of the death to pen Lines Upon the Death of Mr Bruce Reynolds, which he read to the packed, candlelit church, ending with the line: "RIP Gentleman Thief."

Another hero of the punk era, Mick Jones of the Clash, who co-wrote My Daddy was a Bank Robber, was also present but the music was left to the choir and the Alabama Three who sang Too Sick to Pray.

There were a few familiar faces from gangland's past: Freddie "Brown Bread Fred" Foreman and Chris Lambrianou, both of whom were involved with the Krays around the time the robbery took place. Gordon Goody, now very ill in Spain, had sent a message in which he remembered the first meeting of "the most infamous rogues" at a pub in Putney in 1960.

The actor Ray Stevenson read from Kahlil Gibran's The Prophet - "only when you drink from the river

of silence shall you indeed sing" - which was about as far as you can get from Sinatra's "and now the end is near".

Mourners were asked to make a donation to Amnesty International, the organisation to which Reynolds used to send his fees when he wrote occasional pieces for the Guardian.

There was a rendition of Gabriel Faure's In Paradisum and the playing of the familiar Irving Berlin song Let's Face the Music and Dance, a favourite of the robber's, which had also been played at the funeral of his wife, Angela, who died two years ago.

In the epilogue of his memoirs, Reynolds recounted the growing number of funerals he was attending as other train robbers died: Charlie Wilson, shot dead in the south of Spain; Buster Edwards, who hanged himself in south London; Roy James, who had died of a heart attack. He closed the book with a reference to Biggs: "When I look at his frail frame, I see my own mortality. C'est la vie!"

They were the same words with which he greeted Tommy Butler, the detective who eventually arrested him, and they would be on the lips of many of the mourners as they headed for a Shoreditch pub to say a final farewell to Bruce Richard Reynolds.

SECRETS & LIES

The myths and legends of the Great Train Robbery

Over the past fifty years the truth about what actually happened at the Great Train Robbery, and what went on both before and after the robbery, has become slightly fuzzy and out of focus. Some of the things people take for granted as having taken place at the robbery, simply did not happen. Fictional stories about the robbery, both in print and on film and TV, have not helped, and in this era of Wikipedia and Twitter, it is far too easy for people or the media to repeat half-truths and outright lies as the facts they believe to be true.

The robbers have not helped their case, as over the years they have not been averse to telling a few porkies to protect the innocent and not so innocent. Something respected author Piers Paul Read found to his cost when he tried to get the robbers to tell their story in *'The Train Robbers'*.

Names, people and places have been changed over the years. People took responsibility for things they did not do, or helped develop characters that did not exist. As Bruce Reynolds noted, if everyone who claims to have been part of the Great Train Robbery gang, or had been invited to be part of the robbery, had been true, he would have had to borrow Wembley stadium for the gang's meetings.

Ronnie Biggs has had to deal with any number of untruths over the years, and like Reynolds, it was one of the reasons he wrote his autobiography. Both men wanted to put the record straight. Sadly the facts are still often ignored, and many people still think Biggs 'shot' the driver.

We could write an entire book on the myths and legends that surround the Great Train Robbery and the robbers, but here is a quick look at some of the secrets and lies that you may or may not know.

The robbery took place on the night of Thursday, 8 August 1963.
A common mistake that even the producers of *'Mrs Biggs'* series fell for. The robbery happened in the early hours of 8 August. The gang had left Leatherslade Farm around midnight on 7 August and stopped the train just after 3 am on the morning of 8 August. The robbery happened too late for the morning papers, so the first newspaper reports were in the London evening papers of 8 August when £1 million was thought to have been stolen. The first coverage in the national press was on Friday, 9 August.

The robbery took place on Ronnie Biggs' birthday.
True. 8 August 1963 was Biggs' 34th birthday. Biggs was born in 1929. The oldest of the gang at the track was Jimmy White, born in 1920; while the youngest way Roy James, born in 1935.

The main getaway driver was done for dangerous driving just before the robbery.
True. Roy James, who was considered a world class-racing driver, was fined £15 (about £255 in 2013 values), and ordered to pay £15 costs in the County of London Sessions for dangerous driving. This was on 13 June 1963, less than two months before the robbery.

The robbers being robbed stopped the robbery taking place in Surrey.
Partly true. Bruce Reynolds and his firm had looked at a number of trains prior to picking the Glasgow to Euston service, and some of those ran through Surrey. The main target was the 'Money Train' that ran from Bournemouth to Waterloo with a last stop at Weybridge.

The plan was to snatch the bags - around 30 HVP bags, compared to the 120 involved in the Great Train Robbery - from Weybridge station in the early hours. With the plan in place, and all the equipment needed sourced, fate played its hand, as the stolen getaway cars to be used in the assault were themselves stolen from Jimmy White's garage with some of the key equipment needed.

The London Airport robbery was used to finance the Great Train Robbery.
For Bruce Reynolds and his firm the London Airport robbery was just another job. 'I personally invested my own money for the train robbery,' Reynolds explains, 'and it worked out at around 38 quid per head. At the farm for a joke I went around asking for it back, some generously gave me 40 quid saying 'keep the change' some told me to fuck off!' £38 in 1963 would now be worth just over £650.

The 'Ulsterman', or his accomplice, counted the mail bags as they were put on the train in Glasgow and could then tell the gang if the train was worth stopping or not.
A popular myth. Counting the mailbags before the train departed at 6.50 pm would have been of little or no use as only a few bags were put on in Glasgow. Even when the train left Carlisle, just after 9 pm, there were only 30 HVP mailbags on the train. When the train left Warrington, at roughly the same time as the gang left Leatherslade Farm, there were still only 46 HVP bags on the train. The gang had been

at the track for over 30 minutes when the train left Rugby at 2.17 am with the full compliment of 128 HVP mailbags on board. What the accomplice will have known, is how many bags were expected to be loaded on the train that night.

The money was being transported to London to be burnt, as the government could not trust the Scots to do it themselves.
An old wives' tale. All the high value packages on the train originated from banks along the route, most in England, and were being transported to the East Central District Post Office in King Edward Street, London EC1, close to St Paul's. What is true is that the shipment was mainly random bank notes of which the police only had the serial numbers for 15,000 of the £5 notes. That is just £75,000 out of a total of £2,631,784.

Why were there no £10 notes on the train?
At the time of the robbery there were no £10 notes in general circulation. They returned to circulation on 21 February 1964.

I was told that it was not the money the gang was after, but diamonds.
The diamond angle was something Ronnie Biggs came up with for his novel *Keep on Running*, a version that suddenly started being taken seriously with even an Old Bailey judge backing it.

The 'Ulsterman' was the criminal mastermind.
Highly unlikely. The 'Ulsterman' was one of many people who at the time shopped ideas for crimes, or rather the potential financial target for crimes, to known thieves. This was partly due to banks and their safes becoming more secure after the war. In the early 1960s robbers were always on the lookout for information as to when money and valuables were in transit or outside of the bank, and vulnerable.

Brian Field was a much more important figure to the robbery than the 'Ulsterman', while it was Bruce Reynolds, who never met the 'Ulsterman', who developed the plan of the actual robbery with Gordon Goody, Charlie Wilson, John Daily, Buster Edwards and Roger Cordrey. Because of the 'Ulsterman' smokescreen, the police followed and

kept tabs on the 16 Irish men on the train.

Buster coshed the driver.
Ronald Edwards, better known as 'Buster', did not cosh the driver although he did claim to when the publisher of Piers Paul Read's book wanted something new to justify the advance that they were paying to the robbers. Buster also invented the Nazi connection, although he did genuinely know and work with Otto Skorzeny. It was also claimed in November 2012 that Jimmy Hussey had made a deathbed confession that he had hit the driver. He had not.

Ronnie Biggs shot the driver.
No guns were carried or used during the Great Train Robbery. The robbers carried coshes, pick axe handles and an axe, but these were primarily to break into the HVP carriage and intimidate people. The driver got coshed once, and then hit his head on the interior of the cabin. Biggs was not on the train at the time, as he was still on the embankment baby-sitting the back up driver.

The driver Biggs brought along did not know how to drive the train.
A myth. The backup driver knew how to drive an English Electric Class 40 diesel locomotive, but this was one of only a couple of engines that had recently been adapted. The key element was the need for the right pressure in the system to build to release the breaks. This pressure had built up again by the time the train's original driver was put back behind the controls and the backup driver removed.

Compounding the problem was that when the coach had been uncoupled, the stopper had not been fixed back properly on the disconnected vacuum pipe. Jimmy White had raced to the back of the two carriages where he discovered the air pressure valve was not fully closed. After kicking it shut, the train began to move.

Why did the gang have to be so large to tackle just two men?
Over the years people have come to imagine that there were only two people on the train. The driver and his mate. Then they remember that there were five post office sorters working in the HVP carriage.

What is not normally mentioned in stories about the robbery is that when the train was stopped at Sears Crossing there were almost 80 people on board. The most dangerous part of the robbery, from the robbers' point-of-view, was uncoupling the engine and front two carriages from the rest of the train so that the 72 sorters, who could have piled out on to the track at any time, were not alerted to what was going on. These men were never more that 1200 yards from where the front part of the train was sacked at Bridego Bridge.

Scotland Yard were quickly on the scene of the robbery?
The day of the robbery was probably not Scotland Yard's finest. It first received a call about the robbery at 4.25 am. At first they assumed Cheddington Station had been robbed. The first police, from the Buckinghamshire Constabulary, arrived at Cheddington at 4.35 am. At 5.08 am, the first policeman visited the site of the actual robbery. The first official clarification that Scotland Yard had that it was a train robbery only reached them at 10.33 am. Nearly seven hours after the robbery.

The police quickly rounded up the robbers.
As the police files have been opened to the public, it has been remarkable to see just how quickly the authorities had been given the names of some of the robbers. One police officer claims that within twelve hours of the robbery he had been given the names of Reynolds, Daly, Wilson, Welch, Wisbey and Hussey. The first arrest, on 14 August, was more by good luck than good policing, and involved Roger Cordrey whose name was not on any list at the time. Despite having the names, when the trial of the robbers started in January 1964 just nine men from the sixteen at the track, were in the dock, or just over half the participants. The public were not made aware of this.

Not all the Buckinghamshire Constabulary worked the first weekend following the robbery.
True. Just like today, the police force in 1963 was concerned about over spending its budget. So despite the robbery taking place on Thursday many police did not work over that crucial first weekend as the Buckinghamshire Constabulary was concerned about overtime costs. At the time of the robbery, the

Buck's force had 716 officers on its payroll, yet only seven sergeants and 48 constables were actually working at the time the robbery took place.

The robbers left no evidence at the track to connect them with the robbery.
True. The police found no useable evidence at the scene of the robbery. Not at Sears Crossing, Bridego Bridge, or the surrounding area. Not one of the people who came in direct contact with the robbers at the track, of which seven are known, could identify or give any description of the robbers. Even the estimated size of the gang varied in witness statements from 10 to nearly 30.

The fact that the train had been moved from the site of the robbery to Cheddington Station before the police got to look at it, had not helped. The engine was then taken to Crewe before being examined, and not returned to Cheddington until Saturday 10 August, nearly three days after the robbery. That was the first time forensics got to examine it. They only received the clothing that the driver was using at the time of the robbery on 12 August, four and a half days after the robbery.

But I have seen photos of the train on Bridego Bridge.
The famous photos of the train on the bridge is not of the train involved in the robbery (that engine being D326), rather it is D221. For the film *Robbery*, D318 was used as the engine, while for *Buster* it was D306. The train that was at the robbery was also not travelling on the track nearest the embankment, but the Up Fast, which was one track in.

Was the locomotive used at the time of the robbery considered "unlucky".
Unlucky or not, D326 (later renumbered '40126'), the English Electric Class 40 diesel locomotive involved in the Great Train Robbery, certainly had a chequered history.

On Boxing Day 1962, while hauling the Up Midday Scot, D326 ran into the back of the Liverpool – Birmingham Express between Winsford and Crewe at Coppenhall Junction. 18 passengers were killed and 34 injured. After the robbery a secondman was electrocuted in 1964 when working on the engine, while in 1965 the engine had total break failure when entering Birmingham New Street and hits a freight train injuring the guard. It was finally withdrawn from service in February 1985 and quickly cut up for scrap to avoid souvenir hunters.

The robbers dug holes at Leatherslade Farm to hide the mailbags.
Contrary to popular belief the holes dug at the farm were not intended for burying evidence from the train but for food waste. There was an experiment at burning some of the wrappers, but the bags gave off too much smoke.

Why was the farm not burnt down as Reynolds had instructed?
There was never any plan to burn the farm down, merely to remove any evidence that linked the farm to the robbery. This was the money, paper wrappers, mailbags, army fatigues and overalls, plus the vehicles. The plan was for someone - the dustman - to go and remove these items, so that prints or no prints, no one could be tied to the robbery. The experienced robbers were, however, also convinced that they had wiped away all their prints.

Evidence was planted to secure the conviction of an innocent man.
Evidence was almost certainly planted to secure the conviction of an innocent man, only at the time the police did not know he was innocent. The man was Bill Boal who was not one of the train robbery gang but who was helping Roger Cordrey after the event, and was arrested with him while trying to help conceal Cordrey's share of the money. The evidence used to convict Boal, who died in prison, was paint from the farm. The same paint used on Gordon Goody's shoes to convict him. Goody has never denied being one of the train robbers or being at the farm, but he knows those shoes were never near the farm and neither was Boal.

Was other evidence planted to secure a conviction?
Only the people that planted such evidence know for sure, just as Goody knows for sure his shoes were not at the farm. According to Reynolds: 'From the prosecution's position the fingerprints constituted the damning inexplicable proof of guilt against the accused. How can one challenge fingerprint evidence

- what jury would accept that fingerprints had been planted? But the sheer improbability of fifteen professional criminals leaving their fingerprints on the biggest crime they'd been involved in, beggar's belief. Although its not concrete evidence, I had verbal confirmation of malpractice concerning the fingerprint department from ex-police officers serving time."

Why was there no plan for what to do after the robbery?
There was a plan, and that was for each of the robbers to work out how to leave Leatherslade Farm after the money had been counted and divided. Thinking ahead, the gang had taken enough provisions to sit it out at the farm for a couple of weeks if it was felt necessary.

'In hindsight maybe the hideout was a colossal mistake,' Reynolds admits, 'but at the time it seemed the only option that satisfied the majority. The train robbers consisted of two different gangs, neither having worked together before, so there was an element of rivalry and mistrust. When it was suggested that the money should be taken away and divided later - some were against it. So we had to divide the money immediately, where we felt safe. At the time it seemed a better option than risking a mad dash back to London with the money with the danger of potential roadblocks.'

All the robbers got their comeuppance and were brought to justice.
Not exactly. You can argue that for four of the 16 men at the track, or 25 percent of the participants, it was the perfect crime. Three of the main gang, two from Reynolds' firm and one from Roger Cordery's firm, were never caught. They might have been suspected, and even have paid the police to leave them alone, but they were never arrested or charged. The same is true for the back up driver that Biggs brought along. Then there was the 'Ulsterman' and other people who worked behind the scenes who never had their collar felt.

Bruce Reynolds good friend and partner in crime, Terry Hogan, was one of the three to get away?
Reynolds and Hogan worked a lot together over the years, including on the London Airport robbery,

but Hogan felt there was something not quite right about the job that turned out to be the Great Train Robbery. So much so that Hogan was in Cannes, in the south of France, on the day of the robbery and had a watertight alibi. Due to his links to Reynolds he was often pulled in and questioned by the police, but his alibi stood. Hogan helped Reynolds after the robbery, when he was in hiding, and having gone straight and set up a business, he was able to offer Reynolds his first legitimate job when he came out of prison.

Gordon Goody was arrested because somebody thought he was Bruce Reynolds?
True. Goody had travelled to Leicester to visit an old girlfriend. A florist, who delivered flowers to the hotel room, thought Goody was Reynolds as Goody was using glasses similar to Reynolds as a disguise. Goody was arrested and hauled from his bed at 2 am.

The gang members arrested nearly escaped before their trial.
If Bill Boal had not lost his nerve, Wilson, Biggs and Goody and others would have almost certainly have escaped in December 1963 from the hospital wing at HMP Aylesbury. You can read about it in Part Three.

Ronnie Biggs was tried separately from the other robbers?
It was not meant to happen that way, but at the start of the trial a police office let slip in court that Biggs had served times with Reynolds. As a result, Biggs had to be tried separately from the others after the end of the first case. The first case took 51 working days, while Biggs' case took just six days to complete.

Charlie Wilson was already planning to escape from prison when the appeals were being heard.
True. It was the reason that Wilson chose not to appeal against his sentence, as he knew if he was transferred to London for the hearing he might not be returned to HMP Winson Green in Birmingham. The appeals ended on 20 July 1964 and Wilson escaped on 12 August.

Rain stopped Ronnie Biggs' first attempt to escape.
Biggs had to delay his escape from HMP Wandsworth

by 24 hours, as even in light drizzle, hardened criminals were not taken outside to exercise.
'Luckily Paul Seabourne, who was coming to help me escape, knew this too,' explains Biggs. 'Instead Paul used the extra day to remove the mouth and earpieces from the public telephones close to the prison.'

HMP Wandsworth had no alarm linked to the police in case of an escape.
The prison had to ring 999 like anybody else and tell the police switchboard there had been an escape. Questions were asked in Parliament when Biggs went over the wall on 8 July 1965.

What was Prince Carol of Rumania's connection with Ronnie Biggs?
Prince Carol, who died in 2006, was the son of King Carol II of Rumania, and settled in Britain in 1961.

'As far as I know, I never knew and never met Prince Carol,' says Biggs. 'But for some reason once I had escaped the police kept being tipped off that I was hiding in his house.'

On 9 July 1965, the day after the escape, Winterfold House in Cranleigh Surrey, the home of the Prince, was raided by 150 police officers looking for Biggs. The following day the police raided the Upton House Estate in Dorset, which Prince Carol rented from Poole Council.

How do you explain Germany's interest in the Great Train Robbery?
The German interest in the Great Train Robbery started when Stern magazine published the story of the robbery. Much of the information had been supplied by the wife of Brian Field, Karin, who happened to be German. Karin knew more about the robbery then many people suspected.

Due to the positive reaction to the story, it was developed into the TV series *Die Gentlemen bitten zur Kasse (The Gentlemen Require Payment)*, that had a 90% audience share, the highest in German TV history. After that the German press often covered developments in the case.

On Reynolds' capture Frances Reynolds story was

published in Stern, and Buster Edwards famously developed the 'German connection' and Otto Skorzeny, for *The Train Robbers*. The link continues to this day with Biggs having recorded with one of Germany's biggest bands, Die Toten Hosen, while a documentary has recently been made for German television about Nick Reynolds.

I heard that director Stephen Hopkins, the man who came up with *24*, was developing a film or TV series about the Great Train Robbery?
That is true. Back in 2008 Hopkins was involved in developing a project to tell the story through the eyes of the robbers. The project, originally called 'The Robbers' but later *Honour Amongst Thieves*, had the backing of Reynolds and Biggs, and Hopkins met with Reynolds to discuss ideas. At the time all the major UK TV networks and film companies said they had no interest in a project about the train robbery.

Was Bernie Ecclestone the brains behind the Great Train Robbery or one of the three from the gang that got away?
There have been rumours and stories about Bernie Ecclestone and the Great Train Robbery, and he has always treated them in good humour, even being quoted as saying: "There wasn't enough money on that train!"

The connection Ecclestone had to the robbery was a link to the driver Roy James. While in prison James had written to Graham Hill asking for help when he came out. Hill was racing for Brabham, then owned by Ecclestone, and presented James to Ecclestone. He told James he was wasting his time, as he had not been racing for over 10 years. However, Ecclestone had heard that James was a very good silversmith and asked him to make a number of trophies to be used in Formula One. Within weeks James had broken his leg at Abbey Corner while testing a car at Silverstone.

Did Colin Firth have an involvement in the Great Train Robbery?
While it might be romantic to imagine Mr Darcy standing next to Reynolds at the edge of the track, the actor Colin Firth has no links to the Great Train Robbery, other than his name. The name 'Colin

Firth' was one of the aliases given to the Nick, the son of Bruce Reynolds. Bruce and Frances assumed the names of George and Pauline Firth in January 1967, and Nick was 'Colin'.

What about the actress Patsy Kensit?
Actress Patsy Kensit, who was not even born at the time of the robbery, does have a direct link to the Great Train Robbery through her father.

James Kensit, 'Jimmy the Dip', had agreed to be part of Bob Welch's alibi as to what he was up to and where he was at the time of the robbery. Kensit thought better of it and told Scotland Yard that he could not corroborate Welch's story.

And actor Jamie Foreman?
Jamie's connection is his father, Freddie Foreman, who knew Buster Edwards, Charlie Wilson and Bruce Reynolds. Freddie was not involved in the robbery, but helped Buster, Reynolds and Biggs after the robbery. Jamie, best known as Terrence Beesley in *East Enders*, had Buster Edwards as his godfather.

What part did Harrods play in the story of the Great Train Robbery?
Other than Reynolds having certain products bought for him in Harrods while he was in hiding, not a lot. However, after being released from prison Buster Edwards was sent back to prison for six months in October 1975 for shop lifting from Harrods. The kidnappers of Ronnie Biggs also always claimed that Sir Hugh Fraser, who then owned Harrods, financed the kidnapping.

Is it true that Ronnie Biggs is on Twitter?
Ronnie Biggs is on Twitter. If you want to follow him for his updates, he can be found at @RonnieBiggsNews. He is also on Facebook as "ronald.biggs.98", if you want to join his friends.

For other up to date news on Biggs and the Great Train Robbery, visit his web site at www.ronniebiggs.com